Bristow extra!

Frank Dickens

Abelard-Schuman London

An Evening Standard Book

YOU'VE GOT TO HAND IT TO SIR REGINALD.... HE DOES THINK BIG....
RUMOUR HAS IT THAT HE WAS VERY DISAPPOINTED WITH THE CHESTER-PERRY BUILDING WHEN IT WAS FINISHED...
APPARENTLY HE WAS REFUSED PLANNING PERMISSION TO BUILD IT TO THE SIZE HE WANTED.. HAD TO SETTLE FOR SOMETHING MUCH SMALLER...
SCALE 1/10,000!
R.L. CHESTER-P.
4026

I DON'T KNOW WHAT'S THE MATTER WITH ME TODAY...
I'M IN TOO GOOD A MOOD...
DOESN'T MAKE SENSE, THIS FEELING OF CONTENTMENT AND WELL BEING, ON A MONDAY MORNING...
IT'S AS IF I'M SEEING THE PLACE THROUGH ROSE COLOURED SPECTACLES
THINK I'LL TAKE A STROLL...
NOTHING LIKE A TRIP TO THE DIRECTORS' FLOOR TO PUT THINGS IN PERSPECTIVE.........
3846

MY GOD — WHAT A CLIMB...
FOURTEEN FLIGHTS... I'M JUST PAYING A COURTESY VISIT TO THE DIRECTORS' FLOOR..
GASP! GASP!
NO SPECIAL REASON
GOOD POLICY TO LET THEM SEE YOUR FACE OCCASIONALLY......
3847

WHAT A FANTASTIC VIEW THE DIRECTORS HAVE...
PEOPLE SCURRYING ABOUT LIKE ANTS DOWN THERE....
HELLO — THERE'S MY FEATHERED FRIEND SITTING ON MY WINDOW LEDGE....
YOO HOO! I'M UP HERE!
YIPPEE! HE'S SEEN ME......
COME ON, BOY! HIGHER, HIGHER.. KEEP GOING... ONLY TEN MORE FLOORS...
YOU CAN DO IT.: ATTABOY!
GASP!
GOOD LAD.
3848

MUST BE NICE TO BE A BIRD...
TO STAND ON A WINDOW LEDGE, NO MATTER HOW HIGH UP — AND BE ABLE TO LAUNCH YOURSELF INTO SPACE..
WE ARE SEVENTEEN FLOORS UP AT THIS MOMENT, WHICH IS PRETTY HIGH, CONSIDERING, YET TO THIS LITTLE DUMB CREATURE THE HEIGHT MEANS NOTHING..
IN A FEW SECONDS HE'LL FEARLESSLY TAKE OFF AND WHEEL AND CURVE THROUGH THE STILL AIR TO THE STREET BELOW...
GO ON BOY — OFF YOU GO INTO THE WILD BLUE YONDER... ON YOUR MARK — GET SET —
GET OFF! GET OFF!
QUIVER! QUIVER! QUAKE! QUAKE!
3849

HELLO, MR. BRISTOW — WHAT ARE YOU DOING UP ON THE DIRECTORS' FLOOR?
DAMN YOU, LIFTBOY — I HOPED YOU WOULDN'T SPOT ME....
I RATHER PRIDED MYSELF THAT I BLENDED IN, CHAMELEON LIKE, WITH THESE PLUSH SURROUNDINGS.
NO CHANCE — YOU STAND OUT LIKE A SORE THUMB.....
I HATE TO SAY THIS, BUT I SHOULD SAY YOUR BEST BET IS TO STEP INTO MY DINGY LIFT AND LET ME TAKE YOU BACK TO WHERE YOU CAME FROM.
VERY WELL........
THIRD FLOOR, MR. BRISTOW? — MR. BRISTOW? MR. BRISTOW? MR. BRISTOW ???
3850

WELL, WELL, WELL ... SIR REGINALD CHESTER-PERRY'S LATEST ROLLS.....
HELLO, HELLO, HELLO... HAVING A CRAFTY DRINK WHILE THE GOVERNOR'S BACK IS TURNED, EH?
NO FEAR. JUST CHECKING ON THE CONTENTS OF THE BAR....
GLEAM! GLEAM!
GLEAM! GLEAM!
SPARKLE! SPARKLE!
GLITTER! GLITTER!
AWAITING MOET CHANDON DELIVERY
CP1
3912

AND HOW IS SIR REGINALD CHESTER-PERRY, THE FIRM'S FOUNDER, MULTI-MILLIONAIRE AND INDUSTRIAL TYCOON?
HE'S IN ONE OF HIS BAD MOODS, I'M AFRAID.....
THANKS FOR THE WARNING — I'LL TRY AND STAY OUT OF HIS WAY........
GLITTER! GLITTER!
SPARKLE! SPARKLE!
GLEAM! GLEAM!
3913

WHAT'S YOUR TROUBLE?
LEGS. BAD LEGS. HURTS ME TO WALK..
WHAT ABOUT YOU?
NEXT PLEASE
I WAS FIRST!!
I'M BEFORE YOU!!!
BACK, YOU DOGS!!!
SICK BAY
PLEASE BE SEATED
NO SMOKING
SILENCE PLEASE
BAD ARM...CAN'T MOVE IT... AND YOU?
TIRED AND RUN DOWN. NO ENERGY
3780

NEXT PLEASE....
SICK BAY
AH — IT'S MR. POPE, THE FIRM'S HYPOCHONDRIAC. WHAT CAN WE DO FOR YOU?
IT'S MY HEARING. I THINK I'VE GONE DEAF...
COME ALONG, NOW — THERE'S NOTHING WRONG WITH YOUR HEARING... NOR ANY OTHER PART OF YOU FOR THAT MATTER. YOU'RE NOT GETTING ANY TREATMENT OR MEDICINE, SO BE OFF WITH YOU....
QUAVER! QUAVER!
NO MORE TREATMENT OR MEDICINE?
ALACK, ALAS — A BITTER PILL TO SWALLOW........
3781

ANYTHING DOING, NURSE?
SICK BAY
NOT MUCH. OLD POPE WAS IN JUST NOW.
NO SMOKING
WHAT WAS IT THIS TIME?
SAYS HE'S SUDDENLY LOST HIS HEARING....
LOST HIS HEARING, EH? THAT'S A NEW ONE... WHAT DID YOU DO?
I SENT HIM AWAY WITH A FLEA IN HIS EAR.......
NICE ONE SYBIL!
3782

MORNING, MR. POPE... CHEER UP.....
CHEER UP, HE SAYS. WHAT HAVE I TO BE CHEERFUL ABOUT?
I'M NOT WELL AGAIN. I WENT TO THE SICK BAY AND TOLD NURSE MY HEARING WAS A TRIFLE SUSPECT AND SHE LAUGHED ME OUT OF THE BUILDING...
NEVER MIND...IF IT'S ANY CONSOLATION THERE'S A WHISPER GOING ROUND THAT SHE'S BEING TRANSFERRED TO OUR NORTHERN BRANCH...
EH???
I SAID THERE'S A WHISPER GOING AROUND
3783

WELL, WELL — SO MISS SUNMAN IS INTERESTED IN THE TOP TWENTY, EH?
CERTAINLY NOT! P.O.P. STANDS FOR 'PRESERVE OUR PLANET'
IT'S A COMBINED GROUP OF PRESERVATIONISTS AND ECOLOGISTS...
YOU TAKE IT SERIOUSLY?
CERTAINLY! ONLY THIS WEEKEND I WENT OUT ON A DEMO. AT A DETERGENT FACTORY..
TWO HUNDRED OF US WITH BANNERS, FLAGS, LEAFLETS AND PLACARDS PROTESTING AT THE WAY THEY ARE SPOILING OUR COUNTRYSIDE.
HOW DID THE FACTORY REACT?
TYPICALLY.... THEY SET THE DOGS ON US.
HOLY MACKEREL! WHAT DID YOU DO?
WE DROPPED EVERYTHING AND GOT THE HELL OUT OF THERE!
NATCH!
P.O.P.
3804

I HAD NO IDEA YOU WERE A PRESERVATIONIST, MISS SUNMAN....
SOMEBODY HAS TO CARE FOR THE WORLD...SOMEBODY HAS TO THINK OF THE FUTURE...AND THAT'S WHAT 'PRESERVE OUR PLANET' IS ALL ABOUT....
THE TROUBLE IS, THESE DAYS NO ONE GIVES A THOUGHT FOR THE BEAUTIES OF NATURE.. WHERE IS THE GRASS? WHERE ARE THE TREES AND FLOWERS?
P.O.P
COME NOW, MISS SUNMAN... DON'T BE MORBID..... LOOK OUT OF THE WINDOW.....
THERE'S NO USE TRYING TO LOOK OUT OF THAT WINDOW....
THAT FLAMING BIRD IS ALWAYS IN THE WAY!
3805

STRANGE LOOKING BIRD, ISN'T IT?
WHAT DO YOU MEAN — STRANGE?
I'VE NEVER SEEN ANYTHING LIKE IT BEFORE AND I'VE ALWAYS CONSIDERED MYSELF A BIT OF AN ORNITHOLOGIST... WHAT KIND OF BIRD IS IT?
NO IDEA. JUST A COMMON OR GARDEN BIRD AS FAR AS I'M CONCERNED....
WHAT DO YOU CALL HIM?
DODO!!
CHIRP!
3806

THIS P.O.P GROUP OF YOURS— WHAT'S IT ALL ABOUT?
THIS WEEK THE 'PRESERVE OUR PLANET' GROUP ARE TRYING TO BRING PRESSURE TO BEAR AGAINST THE WANTON DESTRUCTION OF TREES....
CONSIDER THE NUMBER OF FORESTS BEING CUT DOWN EVERY DAY TO MAKE PAPER, WHICH WILL BE USED ONCE AND THROWN AWAY.... PAPER BAGS, GIFT WRAPPERS, THAT SORT OF THING.... WE'RE TRYING TO MAKE PEOPLE REALISE HOW UNNECESSARY IT ALL IS.
VERY PRAISEWORTHY INDEED... I'M MOST IMPRESSED.
IMPRESSED ENOUGH TO JOIN US?
CERTAINLY. HOW DO I DO THAT?
SIMPLE!
THERE ARE A NUMBER OF FORMS HERE— IF YOU CAN COMPLETE THEM IN TRIPLICATE........
3807

I'M BEGINNING TO HAVE SECOND THOUGHTS ABOUT JOINING THE 'PRESERVE OUR PLANET' GROUP...
LOOK AT ALL THIS BUMPH I'VE BEEN ASKED TO SEND OUT AS PART OF THIS WEEK'S CAMPAIGN AGAINST THE WANTON DESTRUCTION OF FORESTS....
LEAFLETS, BROCHURES STICKERS — ALL MADE FROM THE VERY TIMBER WE'RE TRYING TO PRESERVE...
THEY DON'T SEEM TO UNDERSTAND WHAT THEY ARE DOING...
THEY CAN'T SEE THE WOOD FOR THE TREES...
3808

THE NEXT OFFICE ON THE RIGHT IS THE BUYING DEPARTMENT. WOULD YOU LIKE TO SEE HOW THEY OPERATE?
WELL, IT'S NOT ON MY ITINERY BUT I'LL CALL IN AND SAY HELLO...
BUYING DEPARTMENT
Z
Z
OH, DEAR— TOO LATE... THE SANDMAN'S BEEN...
3748

WHAT IS YOUR JOB AT CHESTER-PERRY'S?
I'M A BUYING CLERK.
BUYING CLERK?
I ORDER MATERIALS... CHASE UP DELIVERIES...
SOUNDS IMPORTANT.
NOT REALLY. I'M JUST A GLORIFIED PEN-PUSHER...
HOW MUCH WRITING DO YOU DO IN THE COURSE OF A NORMAL WORKING DAY?
NORMAL WORKING DAY? LET'S SEE....
I START BY SIGNING THE LATE-LATE BOOK........
3829

I'M OUT ON MY FEET.. I HARDLY GOT A WINK OF SLEEP LAST NIGHT...
YAWN!
HOW I'M GOING TO GET THROUGH THE NEXT EIGHT HOURS I DON'T KNOW...
HERE WE ARE AT LAST... GOOD JOB I KNOW MY WAY TO WORK BLINDFOLDED....
CHESTER-PERRY BUILDING? TAKE THE SECOND LEFT, FIRST RIGHT.........
3745

YOU LOOK TIRED, THIS MORNING, BRISTOW...
YAWN!
ALL NIGHT POKER SCHOOL.
'MORNING, MR. BRISTOW.. YOU LOOK TIRED.
YAWN!
WINING AND DINING ONE OF THE FAIR SEX.....
'MORNING, MR. BRISTOW. YOU LOOK TIRED.
YAWN!
BURNING THE MIDNIGHT OIL...
YOU LOOK TIRED, BRISTERS.
POSTBOY
YAWN!
UP ALL NIGHT AT A DISCO....
3746

PENNY FOR THEM, SMITTY..
THE OTHER DAY I READ AN ARTICLE ABOUT TAKING STOCK OF ONE'S LIFE...
THIS'LL BE HEAVY..
IT SAID THE FIRST STEP IS TO STAND BEFORE A MIRROR AND TAKE A HARD LOOK AT YOURSELF.....
THIS MORNING I DECIDED TO TRY IT, SO I STOOD BEFORE A MIRROR AND LOOKED SEARCHINGLY AT MY FACE....
AND YOUR CONCLUSIONS?
NONE — COULDN'T SEE MYSELF.... MY EYES WERE TOO FULL OF TEARS.....
3918

DON'T SPEAK TO ME....
YOU AND YOUR STUPID THEORIES....
'TAKE ANOTHER LOOK IN THE MIRROR' YOU SAID, 'FIRST THING IN THE MORNING IS NOT THE BEST TIME TO TAKE STOCK OF ONE'S LIFE. LET THE DAY SMOOTH OUT THOSE FURROWS AND WRINKLES'
SO I TRIED IT... GOT HOME LAST NIGHT, PICKED UP A MIRROR — AND WHAT DID I SEE? PIGGY LITTLE EYES, A BULBOUS NOSE, LOOSE LIPS AND A SAGGING JAW — ASSEMBLED IN A FACE LIKE A PRUNE
I WAS SO UPSET I DASHED THE MIRROR TO THE GROUND....
ON TOP OF EVERYTHING ELSE — SEVEN YEARS BAD LUCK!!!
3920

FREDERICK J FUDGE CHIEF BUYER
BUMP!
YES, MR. FUDGE... I'LL ATTEND TO IT AT ONCE.....
FREDERICK J FUDGE CHIEF BUYER
OW! OW! OW! OW!
EIGHT YEARS I'VE BEEN HERE AND I STILL HAVEN'T MASTERED THE ART OF BACKING OUT OF HIS OFFICE.....
4047

WELL GENTLEMEN— WHAT'S IT TO BE ?
WHO KNOWS ? THE STATE THESE MENU CARDS ARE IN!
THEY ARE INDECIPHERABLE...
TELL YOU WHAT LET'S PLAY POT LUCK.
I'LL HAVE WHATEVER'S WRITTEN UNDER THIS BLOB OF CUSTARD...
I'LL TAKE WHATEVER'S WRITTEN UNDER THIS TOMATO KETCHUP
I'LL TAKE THE GRAVY STAIN
BAGS I THE GREASY THUMBPRINT...
4070

MR. GORDON BLUE — A WORD WITH YOU...
IF IT IS ABOUT TODAYS LUNCH I CAN EXPLAIN EVERYTHING.... THERE WAS A POWER CUT— THE FRIDGE BROKE DOWN.. THE OVEN ——
IT'S ABOUT THE STATE OF THE MENU CARDS. THEY ARE SO STAINED IT IS DISGUSTING. EVEN YOUR MOST HARDENED CUSTOMERS ARE COMPLAINING. I HAVE HERE A PETITION SIGNED BY ALL YOUR REGULARS..
BUT I CANNOT READ A WORD...
SORRY ABOUT THAT— —LEAKY PEN!
4071

WATCH OUT— HERE COMES TROUBLE....
WHISK! WHISK!
WHICH ONE OF THOSE STUPID TYPISTS IS RESPONSIBLE FOR TYPING OUT MY NEW MENU....?
SHE'S LEFT THE KIDNEYS OUT OF THE STEAK AND KIDNEY PIE.... SHE'S LEFT AN 'S' OUT OF POISSON... SHE'S WRITTEN 'BANGERS AND MUSH'..'YORKSHIRE PADDING' AND 'KNICKER BOCKER GORY..
OBVIOUSLY A REGULAR CUSTOMER.......
4072

ONE UP TO ME...
I'VE JUST BEEN TO SEE MR. GORDON BLUE, OUR MASTER CHEF, TO COMPLAIN ABOUT THE STAINS ON HIS MENU CARDS...
'I DENY IT' HE SAID.....
EVERYTHING IN MY CANTEEN CONFORMS TO THE HIGHEST STANDARDS OF CLEANLINESS AND HYGIENE'...
'OH, YEAH' I SAID —AND PRODUCED ONE FROM MY POCKET....
LEFT HIM STANDING THERE WITH EGG ALL OVER HIS FACE...
4073

4074
WHY IS MR. GORDON BLUE LOOKING SO SMUG?
IT'S THE FIRST DAY OF HIS NEW MENU CARDS... THOSE OLD ONES FINALLY MADE THE DUSTBIN...
STAND ASIDE, LADIES... LET ME SEE HOW MY CUSTOMERS ARE APPRECIATING MY LATEST EFFORTS TO GIVE THEM SATISFACTION.....
PASS THE TOMATO SAUCE...
BAGS THE COFFEE
TOMATO KETCHUP
MIND IF I DIP THIS END IN YOUR GRAVY...?
HOW ABOUT A LITTLE CUSTARD?
I'LL TRY SOME OF THE SOUP OF THE DAY.

POSTBOY
ER- MR. BRISTOW... SORRY TO DISTURB YOU...
EH. WHAT? WHAT? WHERE AM I?
YOU WERE ASLEEP
NONSENSE! WHAT DO YOU WANT, ANYWAY?
CAN YOU — WITH A CLEAR CONSCIENCE — DO NOTHING ALL WEEK AND ACCEPT YOUR WAGES ON FRIDAY?
CAN A FISH SWIM?
3893

THANK GOD, ANOTHER DAY OVER...
O.K... LET'S GO!
THERE'S NO RUSH — WE WON'T GET OUT ANY QUICKER.
YOU KNOW.... THIS SHOULDN'T BE NECESSARY IN THIS DAY AND AGE......
TOLL 1p
FUMBLE! FUMBLE! FUMBLE! FUMBLE!
4053

SOME ENCHANTED EVENING....
YOU'RE RIGHT, BRISTOW...
STATION
HOW PLEASANT TO TAKE A LEISURELY STROLL TO THE STATION — THE PRESSURES OF THE DAY BEHIND ONE AND A FEELING OF TOTAL RELAXATION...
I SUPPOSE EVERYONE THAT'S HAD A HARD DAY MUST FEEL AS WE DO... AT PEACE WITH THE WORLD...
SOME ENCHANTED EVENING....
STAFF ROOM
BRITISH HI-SPEED RAIL REGRET EXTENSIVE DELAYS DUE TO : Euphoria
4054

ISN'T IT MARVELLOUS — THERE'S ALWAYS SOME LOUDMOUTH GOES AND SPOILS EVERYTHING...
HERE WE ARE, RELAXING AFTER A HARD DAY AND WE HAVE TO PUT UP WITH THAT......
BUFFET BLAH! BLAH! BLAH! BLAH!
STUCK IN A RAT HOLE OF AN OFFICE WITH A BUNCH OF HALF-WITTED IMBECILES ON THE ONE HAND AND A CROWD OF PATHETIC MORONS ON THE OTHER...
BUFFET !
FUNNY HOW PETERSON OF PUBLIC RELATIONS IS ATTRACTED TO THAT FAIR HAIRED BARMAID....
BLAH! BLAH! BLAH! BLAH!
4055

YOU KNOW, BRISTOW...THIS IS SUCH A LOVELY EVENING I SHALL BE ALMOST SORRY WHEN MY TRAIN COMES...
HERE IT COMES — ON YOUR FEET....
PERHAPS I'LL LET THIS ONE GO — WAIT FOR THE NEXT....
DON'T TALK NONSENSE... GET ON THE TRAIN...
BUT IT'S SO PLEASANT HERE... MUST I? NEED I?
FOR PETE'S SAKE JONES — GET ON THE BLASTED TRAIN..
THIS IS SHAPING UP LIKE A SCENE FROM 'BRIEF ENCOUNTER'....
4056

DAMN! DAMN! DAMN!
I POP ROUND THE CORNER TO BUY AN EVENING PAPER AND MISS MY TRAIN.... NOW I HAVE TO WAIT FOR THE 6:30....
NUISANCE, REALLY... I WANTED TO TRAVEL BACK WITH THE 'FINISH IT BEFORE I LEAVE TONIGHT' CROWD..
NOW I'M STUCK WITH THE 'OUR DINNERS ARE IN THE OVEN' GANG.....
4057

KEEPING YOU BUSY, MR. PERKINS?
BUSY? YOU CAN SAY THAT AGAIN.....
BRITISH HI-SPEED RAIL
IF IT'S NOT POLISHING AND DUSTING AND CLEANING THE STATION, IT'S PUNCHING TICKETS AND WAVING FLAGS..
AND WHAT WITH TRAINS ARRIVING AND LEAVING EVERY FEW MINUTES WE DON'T GET A MOMENT'S PEACE....
HELLUVA WAY TO RUN A RAILROAD.....
3760

I CAN'T WORK UNDER THESE CONDITIONS JONES... NOT WITH OLD FUDGE KEEPING HIS EYE ON US THE WHOLE TIME....
I SUGGEST WE COME OUT ON STRIKE....
LOOK OUT— HE'S GOT HIS EYE ON US RIGHT NOW...
IT'S O.K...HE'S GOING OUT OF THE ROOM....
THAT'S IT, THEN— ALL OUT ON STRIKE....
STRIKE WHILE THE EYE ON IS NOT!
GROAN! KINDLY LEAVE THE STAGE.....
3787

THAT'S IT THEN — WE'RE COMING OUT ON STRIKE FOR BETTER WORKING CONDITIONS.
RIGHT.
SOLIDARITY—THAT'S THE KEY...
ALL FOR ONE, ONE FOR ALL, 'CETRA...
RIGHT. WE'RE OFF! STOP WRITING. PUT YOUR PEN DOWN.
AFTER YOU.
NO. YOU FIRST.
BAGS YOU START.
NO—YOU.
AGE BEFORE BEAUTY
CART BEFORE THE HORSE
DIRT BEFORE THE BROOM.
SHOWERS BEFORE FLOWERS...
3788

WHAT'S ALL THIS ABOUT A STRIKE?
WE'RE STRIKING AGAINST THE MANAGEMENT.
WE'RE FIGHTING FOR BETTER WORKING CONDITIONS... PARITY WITH THE NORTHERN BRANCH... AN IMPROVEMENT IN MANAGEMENT WORKER RELATIONSHIPS... AN INCREASE IN OVERTIME RATES...
IS JONES IN ON THIS?
OF COURSE HE IS, DUM DUM...
HE'S OUR SPOKESMAN!
SPEAKING...
3789

O.K. JONES — FUDGE WILL BE HERE IN A MINUTE. DOWN TOOLS.
HOW ARE WE GOING TO PUT IT TO HIM..?
SIMPLY TELL HIM WE'RE STRIKING FOR BETTER WORKING CONDITIONS.
AS LONG AS WE STICK TOGETHER WE'VE GOT HIM OVER A BARREL. WHAT CAN HE SAY?
PICK UP THOSE PENS AND GET ON WITH YOUR WORK!
INVOICE NUMBER 42893/7
INVOICE NUMBER 82341/6....
3790

YIPPEE! I'M FULL OF THE HOLIDAY SPIRIT...
CLICK!
BLUE SKIES... GOLDEN SANDS... SPARKLING WAVELETS..
SOUNDS LOVELY. WHEN DO YOU GO?
LAST TWO WEEKS OF SEPTEMBER.
OH, WHAT A BEAUTIFUL MORNIN...
LAST TWO...??
3791

HEY — WHAT HAVE WE HERE?
MY FEATHERED FRIEND IS BACK FROM HIS SOJOURN IN THE SUN...
MY WORD, HE LOOKS EXHAUSTED...
PROBABLY BEEN FIGHTING A HEADWIND·FOR DAYS ON END....
AAAH, POOR THING... EVEN THOUGH HE'S AT THE END OF HIS TETHER HE'S TRYING TO GREET ME...
CROAK! CROAK! CROAK! CROAK!
OR IS HE?
SOUNDS MORE LIKE 'O FOR THE WINGS OF A DOVE....'
CROAK! CROAK! CROAK!
4034

AH, SPRING — GLORIOUS SPRING, TRA LA....
BLUE SKIES... FLUFFY WHITE CLOUDS AND TREES HEAVY WITH BLOSSOM...
MOTHER NATURE'S YEARLY MIRACLE, TRA LA..
WHAT'S ALL THIS TRA LA ?
TRAINS LATE!
STATION
BRITISH HI-SPEED RAIL REGRET EXTENSIVE DELAYS DUE TO:
Lambs gambolling on line...
4035

WHAT A BEAUTIFUL DAY...
GLORIOUS DAY
ISN'T IT LOVELY?
JERK!
HOW PLEASANT TO FEEL THE SUN AGAIN
ONE OF THOSE DAYS THAT MAKES YOU GLAD TO BE ALIVE....
WINTER IS BEHIND US NOW...
WILL SOMEBODY SHUT THAT BLASTED WINDOW!!
4036

WHAT A GLORIOUS DAY... GOOD TO BE ALIVE ON A DAY LIKE THIS...
SPRING IS IN THE AIR.... NO DOUBT ABOUT IT...
MORNING, MR. FUDGE— BEAUTIFUL DAY...
AND A HEY AND A HO AND A HEY NONNY NO TO YOU TOO.........
SLAM!
4037

I SAY, BRISTOW.....
SSH!
GRUNT! GRUNT! HEAVE! HEAVE!
IT'S ABOUT —
SSH!
HEAVE! GRUNT! HEAVE!
WHAT'S GOING ON?
LISTEN — CAN YOU HEAR THAT?
HEAVE! GRUNT! HEAVE!
WHAT THE DEVIL IS IT?
THE FIRST SOUNDS OF SPRING
GRUNT! GRUNT! HEAVE! HEAVE!
THE TRAFFIC WARDENS SHED THEIR WINTER COATS.......
SIGH!
4038

THIS IS VERY PLEASANT, BRISTOW... THE STIRRING OF THE BLOOD AND QUICKENING OF THE PULSE, WITH THE REALISATION THAT SPRING IS HERE...
I LOVE THE EARLY MONTHS... WHEN CROCUSES, SNOWDROPS AND DAFFODILS SHOW THEIR PRETTY FACES.... WHEN TREES GAILY CLOTHE THEMSELVES IN THEIR GREENERY AND TINY LAMBS GAMBOL IN THE MEADOWS..
WHAT'S YOUR FAVOURITE MONTH?
ANY MONTH WITH FIVE PAYDAYS IN IT........
4039

HOW MESSRS GUN & FAMES GET SO FAR BEHIND WITH THEIR WORK IS BEYOND ME..
LOOK AT THIS ORDER... THEY PROMISED DELIVERY LAST OCTOBER...
HALLO — THIS IS BRISTOW OF CHESTER-PERRYS.... IT'S ABOUT OUR ORDER.....
SORRY, MR BRISTOW — COULD YOU CALL BACK..?
WE'RE JUST TAKING DOWN OUR CHRISTMAS DECORATIONS......
4040

Scene: The offices of Daily Things.
'MORNING JOHN...
'MORNING CHUCK..
IS THERE ANYTHING ON THE WIRE?
TOP POLITICIAN'S STRANGE HOBBY.. AMAZING REVELATIONS...
ANYTHING ELSE?
POLICE CHIEF EXPOSED AS HATCHET FIEND...
NOTHING ELSE?
ROYAL FAMILY IN NIGHT CLUB BRAWL..
YOUR FRIEND, SIR REGINALD CHESTER-PERRY HAS ARRIVED BACK FROM HIS CARIBBEAN CRUISE
HOLD THE FRONT PAGE!!!
4017

WELL, WELL — SIR REGINALD CHESTER-PERRY BACK FROM HIS CARIBBEAN CRUISE, EH?
GLITTER! GLITTER!
GLEAM! GLEAM
FR
THE WHOLE FAMILY ARRIVED THIS MORNING...
YOU DON'T LOOK VERY BROWN AFTER THREE MONTHS IN THE SUN...
HE WOULDN'T TAKE ME, A CHAUFFEUR, ON A CRUISE — WOULD HE?
DOES HE LET YOU USE THE CAR WHILST HE'S ON HOLIDAY?
NO—BUT WHILE THE CAT'S AWAY,
NUDGE NUDGE
YOU DON'T MEAN—?
TOO TRUE
WEDDINGS, FUNERALS, REMOVALS, MINI-CABBING....
GLEAM! GLEAM!
GLITTER! GLITTER!
4018

WHAT'S SIR REGINALD CHESTER-PERRY LIKE? WHAT KIND OF MAN IS OUR BELOVED FIRM'S FOUNDER?
SIR REGINALD? GOD BLESS HIM! THE FINEST BOSS A MAN EVER HAD....
IS HE AS STERN AND UNYIELDING AS THEY MAKE HIM OUT TO BE?
NO. COMPLETE OPPOSITE... CHARMING FELLOW...
I'VE SEEN HIM ON THE BOX A FEW TIMES BUT I'VE NEVER SEEN HIM SMILE. DOES HE HAVE A SENSE OF HUMOUR?
MARVELLOUS SENSE OF HUMOUR..
YOU SHOULD JUST HEAR HIM LAUGHING IN BED AROUND NINE O'CLOCK ON A RAINY MONDAY MORNING.........
WE ARE NOT AMUSED!
4019

TELL ME MORE ABOUT OUR BELOVED FIRM'S FOUNDER... I MEAN - TAKE THIS EVENING, WHEN HE COMES OUT OF THE BUILDING, WILL HE SPEAK TO YOU?

HE'LL NOD AS I OPEN THE DOOR BUT THAT'S ALL....
I SHALL TUCK THE RUG AROUND HIS KNEES, LIGHT HIS CIGAR, SWITCH ON THE STEREO AND HAND HIM HIS COPIES OF 'DAILY THINGS' AND 'FINANCIAL PRATTLE'....

THEN WE SHALL DRIVE OFF SMOOTHLY AND COMFORTABLY IN THE DIRECTION OF DUNWELL MANOR....
SIGH! WHAT A WONDERFUL PICTURE YOU PAINT...

I SHALL CHERISH THAT IMAGE TONIGHT AS I FIGHT MY WAY ON TO THE MISERY LINE.....
4020

WHAT A FOOL I'VE BEEN
I COULD HAVE BEEN UP THERE WITH SIR REGINALD AND THE LIKES, IF I'D LISTENED TO MY DEAR OLD FATHER.....

"GET A TRADE," HE SAID, "GET A TRADE AND YOU'LL ALWAYS HAVE SOMETHING TO FALL BACK ON...."

AND WHAT DID I DO? INSTEAD OF TAKING HIS ADVICE I FRITTERED AWAY MY YOUTH....

NOW, WHEN I SHOULD BE AT THE TOP OF THE TREE.....
BRAIN SURGERY FOR BEGINNERS
4021

WITH A NINE-TO-FIVE JOB WHAT'S THE FIRST THING YOU DO WHEN YOU COME INTO THE OFFICE IN THE MORNING....?

LOOK AT THE CLOCK, OF COURSE....

EVERYBODY DOES THAT..... WHAT'S THE NEXT THING?

PUSH THE BIG HAND BACK TO THE TWELVE, DUM DUM..
4043

STOP WORK, BRISTOW— EVERYONE IS WANTED DOWN IN RECEPTION...
FIRE DRILL?
NO...
BOMB SCARE?
NO...
MISS SHARMAN OF THE TYPING POOL IS BEING GIVEN A PUBLIC REPRIMAND...
HOLY MACKEREL! WHAT'S SHE DONE?
SHE WAS CAUGHT SNEAKING OUT AT THREE O'CLOCK WITH THE PART TIMERS...
4005

WOW! WHAT A HARROWING ORDEAL.....
THAT'S THE FIRST PUBLIC REPRIMAND I'VE ATTENDED SINCE I'VE BEEN WITH THIS FIRM...AND I HOPE IT'S THE LAST...
AFTER ALL, TRYING TO SNEAK OUT AT THREE O'CLOCK WITH THE PART TIMERS ISN'T SO TERRIBLE...WE'VE ALL TRIED IT AT SOME TIME...
I THINK 40 DAYS HARD LABOUR AND LOSS OF PRIVILEGES IS A VERY HARSH SENTENCE...
I AGREE... WHAT EXACTLY IS LOSS OF PRIVILEGES?
NO TEA AND CAKES
MAN'S INHUMANITY TO MAN...
4006

THINK I'LL NIP INTO THE TYPING POOL AND FIND OUT HOW MISS SHARMAN IS TAKING HER 40 DAYS HARD LABOUR...
AFTERNOON, MISS SHARMAN.....
CAN'T STOP, MR. BRISTOW...
ONLY THIRTY NINE DAYS TO GO... WHAT EXACTLY DO YOU HAVE TO DO?
TAKATAK TAKATAKA TAKATAKA DING!
TAKATATAKA TAKATAKA TAKATAK DING!
TYPING, TYPING, TYPING... FROM THE MOMENT I ARRIVE IN THE MORNING TILL THE TIME I LEAVE... TYPING, TYPING, TYPING...
BUT THAT'S YOUR NORMAL JOB...WHAT'S THE HARD LABOUR BIT?
TAKATAKA TAKATAK DING!
THEY CONFISCATE YOUR CARBON PAPER....
TAKATAKATAKA TING! TAKATAKATAK TING! TAKATAKATAK TING! TAKATAKATAK
TAKATAK A TAK A TAK DING!
4007

ARE WE AGREED?
AGREED!
RIGHT! WHAT SHALL WE SAY?
LETTER TO THE MANAGEMENT DEAR SIRS,
WE, THE UNDERSIGNED, FEEL THAT THE SENTENCE OF 40 DAYS HARD LABOUR IMPOSED UPON MISS SHARMAN OF THE TYPING POOL IS BARBARIC IN THE EXTREME.
IT IS OUR CONSIDERED OPINION THAT A YOUNG, DELICATELY NURTURED GIRL LIKE MISS SHARMAN WILL NOT HAVE THE STRENGTH TO WITHSTAND THE RIGOURS OF NON-STOP TYPING FOR THIS PERIOD. WE DEMAND THEREFORE THAT THIS SENTENCE BE SUSPENDED...
MISS SHARMAN — WILL YOU TYPE THIS OUT AT ONCE —
3 COPIES...
SOB!
4008

CHEER UP, HICKFORD — WHY SO GLUM?
I'M WORKING HARD ON THE BUMPER SPRING NUMBER OF THE CHESTER-PERRY HOUSE JOURNAL... AND FRANKLY, I'M WORRIED...
THIS PARTICULAR ISSUE IS VERY HEAVY READING, CONTAINING, AS IT DOES, FULL DETAILS OF COMPANY POLICIES AND REPORTS..
HOW CAN WE PICK UP NEW READERS WITH THAT KIND OF MATERIAL?
EASY PEASY....
FREE WITH EVERY COPY — AN 'I HATE CHESTER-PERRY' TEE SHIRT.....
4042

WELL, WELL — MISS SHARMAN OF THE TYPING POOL....
IT'S THE TENTH DAY OF YOUR 40 DAYS HARD LABOUR, IS IT NOT?
HOW DOES IT FEEL TO BE TYPING NON STOP FROM MORNING TILL NIGHT?
NOT TOO BADLY, THANKS. IT'S MERELY A QUESTION OF ESTABLISHING A ROUTINE AND STICKING TO IT. I AM FULLY CONFIDENT THAT AT THE END
-TING! -TING! -TING! -TING! -TING!
4009

Scene: The Cellars of the Bodega Brothers, Wine Merchants (Purveyors to the Nobility)
ALACK! ALAS
GENTLEMEN— FOR SOME REASON OR OTHER OUR SALES THIS SUMMER HAVE REACHED THEIR LOWEST EVER.
IT IS WITH SOME RELUCTANCE, THEREFORE THAT WE ARE FORCED TO CLOSE DOWN THE BUSINESS AND DECLARE YOU ALL REDUNDANT.
RING! RING! RING! RING!
BODEGA BROTHERS, WINE MERCHANTS
WHAT— CHESTER-PERRY'S?..... FACTORY OUTING TO THE SEASIDE? SUFFICIENT DRINKS FOR THREE COACHES? YES SIR— CERTAINLY SIR— THANK YOU SIR!
CLICK!
BUSINESS AS USUAL LADS!!!
PRAISE BE— A MIRACLE!
HALLELUJAH
3894

ARE WE FIT THEN, SIR?
#economy
LET ME SEE... THE CRATES OF LIGHT AND BROWN ALES ARE IN THE BOOT OF THE FIRST COACH. SPIRITS AND SPLITS ARE IN THE SECOND AND WE'VE THREE BARRELS OF BITTER HERE.....
JUST THE THREE BARRELS, SIR?
CHESTER-PERRY WORKS OUTING
THREE IT IS. LET'S GO. WHERE'S OUR FIRST STOP?
MAY I SUGGEST THE OFF-LICENCE?
RIGHT ON BROTHER!
3895

WHAT'S THE MATTER WITH BRISTOW THIS MORNING?
HE'S SULKING BECAUSE THE FACTORY HAVE GONE ON THEIR ANNUAL COACH OUTING AND HE HAS TO STAY HERE AND WORK — EXCUSE ME...
THEY'VE GONE NOW — FOR HEAVEN'S SAKE STOP GRIZZLING!!
SNIVEL! SNIVEL! SNIVEL!
3896

'MORNING, MR. GORDON BLUE — HOW'S OUR MASTER CHEF AWOURD HUI?
CONTENTED.....
I HAVE PREPARED THE PACKED LUNCHES FOR THE FACTORY COACH OUTING.... EACH ONE A MASTERPIECE IN ITSELF...
THE MIND BOGGLES...
COLD ROAST TURKEY AND WATERCRESS... CRAB AND MAYONNAISE...... TENDER PIECES OF SMOKED SALMON REVERENTLY PLACED BETWEEN THIN SLICES OF NEWLY BAKED BROWN BREAD..
THE MOUTH WATERS...
MEANWHILE : ON A COAST BOUND COACH.....
PASS THE TOMATO KETCHUP..
PASS THE TOMATO KETCHUP.
SWIZZ! I FANCIED DRIPPING!
Hireconomy Coaches
PASS THE TOMATO KETCHUP
AFTER YOU WITH THE TOMATO KETCHUP
3897

MORNING, CHARLIE.... HOW DID THE CHESTER-PERRY FACTORY OUTING GO?
GREAT... BEST YET.
WHAT WAS THE WEATHER LIKE?
IDEAL..
PLENTY TO DRINK?
I'LL SAY....
HOW WAS MUDSEA?
NEVER GOT THERE.
AT HALF WAY HOUSE WE RAN INTO THE MYLES AND RUDGE FACTORY OUTING........
SHINER! SHINER!
'NUFF SAID...
3898

... AND HERE WE HAVE THE CHESTER-PERRY BUYING DEPARTMENT, UNDER MR. FUDGE... RUNS LIKE CLOCKWORK.....
BUT LOOK AT THE TIME — AND THEY ARE ALL SITTING THERE MOTIONLESS....
IT'S EARLY YET... IT'S ONLY 9.30.....
THEY'RE WAITING FOR SOMEONE TO WIND THEM UP........
4044

THERE IT IS — THE PERFECT PEACH MELBA... PEACHES, ICE CREAM AND MELBA SAUCE.... IF MUSIC BE THE FOOD — EAT ON!
MR. GORDON BLUE — CONGRATULATIONS! CONGRATULATIONS!!!
OUR CANTEEN HAS BEEN UPGRADED TO FOUR STAR RATING IN THE 'GOOD CANTEEN GUIDE 1974'
NIRVANA!!
NEXT STOP — THE SAVOY!
EUPHORIA!
EUPHORIA!
EUPHORIA!
EUPHORIA!
EUPHORIA!
EUPHORIA!
3993

WHERE ARE YOU EATING TODAY?
CANTEEN, OF COURSE...
OUR MASTER CHEF, MR. GORDON BLUE IS CELEBRATING...
APPARENTLY WE'VE BEEN UPGRADED TO FOUR STARS IN THE 'GOOD CANTEEN GUIDE 1974'....
LET'S HOPE IT HASN'T GONE TO HIS HEAD...
YOU WERE SAYING...... ??
MR. GORDON BLUE INVITES YOU TO A CELEBRATION LUNCH
DRESS: WHITE TIE
3994

HOW NICE IT IS TO SEE OUR MASTER CHEF SO HAPPY...
WELL — IT'S NOT EVERYDAY ONE IS UPGRADED TO FOUR STARS IN THE 'GOOD CANTEEN GUIDE 1974'
IN HONOUR OF THE OCCASION MR. GORDON BLUE HAS DEVISED A COMPLETELY FRENCH MENU (FRANCE BEING THE HOME OF GASTRONOMY).... THEY STARTED WITH SOUP A' L'OIGNON, FOLLOWED THAT WITH SOLE VERONIQUE AND ARE NOW ON THEIR MAIN COURSE, WHICH CELEBRATES OUR FOUR STARS...
STAND ASIDE, LADIES — LET ME SEE HOW MY CLIENTELE ARE ENJOYING THEIR BOEUF QUATRE ETOILES...
DONNEZ-MOI LE TOMATO KETCHUP...
APREZ-VOUS AVEC LE TOMATO KETCHUP
AVEC TOMATO KETCHUP C'EST DELICIEUX!
MOI AUSSI
COCHONS!
TOMATO KETCHUP S'IL VOUS PLAIT...
3995

YOU'VE GOT TO HAND IT TO MR. GORDON BLUE, OUR MASTER CHEF.....
HE'S DONE WELL TO WIN AN EXTRA STAR IN THE 'GOOD CANTEEN GUIDE 1974'
IT'S BEYOND ME...TO TELL YOU THE TRUTH I'VE NEVER RATED GORDON BLUE'S COOKING AT ALL....
IF LAST YEAR HIS DREADFUL COOKING RATED THREE STARS WHAT KIND OF PLACES RATE ONLY ONE STAR?
HOT DOG STALLS....... CHESTNUT BRAZIERS....... MOTORWAY RESTAURANTS...
3996

HE'S DONE IT THIS TIME... HE'S OVER-REACHED HIMSELF... BUT HE'LL BE SORRY...
WHO'S DONE IT THIS TIME? WHO'S OVER-REACHED HIMSELF? WHO'LL BE SORRY?
MR. GORDON BLUE -OUR MASTER CHEF...
WHAT'S HE DONE?
ON THE STRENGTH OF HIS BEING UPGRADED IN THE 'GOOD CANTEEN GUIDE 1974' HE'S INCREASED HIS PRICES....
SO?
SO EVERYONE IS GOING TO BOYCOTT THE PLACE...
HE HAS ONLY HIMSELF TO BLAME. A CHEF SHOULD STICK TO HIS POTS AND LEAVE MONEY MATTERS TO OTHERS..
YOU MEAN AS A BUSINESSMAN HE'S COOKED HIS OWN GOOSE?
3997

MR. GORDON BLUE — WITH RESPECT, I THINK YOU'RE A DUM DUM....
DUM DUM?
I UNDERSTAND YOU HAVE INCREASED ALL THE PRICES IN THE CANTEEN....
CERTAINLY! WE HAVE BEEN UPGRADED IN THE 'GOOD CANTEEN GUIDE 1974'
BUT I UNDERSTAND THAT FOR THE PAST WEEK PEOPLE HAVE STAYED AWAY FROM THE CANTEEN.....
FOOLS!
IF THE BOYCOTT CONTINUES HOW CAN YOU POSSIBLY HOPE TO SHOW A PROFIT?
IMBECILE — I SHALL COOK THE BOOKS!
3998

COME ON, TRAIN — COME ON! LOOK AT THE TIME....
EXCUSE ME... MR BRISTOW, ISN'T IT?
THAT'S RIGHT...
AMAZING — I NEVER FORGET A FACE....
YOU WORK FOR THE CHESTER-PERRY ORGANISATION... BUYING DEPARTMENT.
THAT'S RIGHT — WHO ARE YOU THEN?
MY NAME'S PRINGLE... I WORK FOR PONSONBY'S PERMANENT POSITIONS... SURELY YOU REMEMBER ME? I GOT YOU THE JOB WITH CHESTER-PERRY'S...
MAY GOD HAVE MERCY ON YOUR SOUL...........
4029

Scene: The offices of PONSONBY'S PERMANENT POSITIONS ('OUR FACES FIT!')
'MORNING MR. PRINGLE
'MORNING GIDEON
WHAT'S SO FUNNY?
ANYONE I KNOW?
I BUMPED INTO AN OLD CLIENT OF OURS ON THE STATION....
NO. BEFORE YOUR TIME. CHAP CALLED BRISTOW. I FIXED HIM UP AT CHESTER-PERRY'S..........
IS HE HAPPY THERE?
WHO CARES? WE GOT OUR COMMISSION, DIDN'T WE?
DON'T YOU EVER HAVE QUALMS WHEN YOU PLACE AN OBVIOUS SQUARE PEG IN A ROUND HOLE?
QUALMS? QUALMS??? SNAP OUT OF IT, GIDEON...
THIS IS NO JOB FOR A MAN WITH A CONSCIENCE.....
4030

MORNING, BRISTOW... YOU LOOK PREOCCUPIED
HARDLY SURPRISING. DO YOU KNOW WHO I MET THIS MORNING? THE MAN THAT GOT ME THIS JOB.
EVEN HAD THE NERVE TO REMIND ME! I'LL GIVE HIM PONSONBY'S PERMANENT POSITIONS IF I EVER SEE HIM AGAIN....
GOOD HEAVENS — YOU DON'T MEAN THAT SWINE PRINGLE!!
HE'S RESPONSIBLE FOR MY YEARS OF MISERY. I DIDN'T WANT AN OFFICE JOB BUT HE TALKED ME INTO IT...
HE'S PROBABLY DONE THE SAME THING TO THOUSANDS OF OTHER POOR DEVILS....
MY GOD — HE HAS A LOT TO ANSWER FOR......
4031

Scene: The offices of Ponsonby's Permanent Positions ('Our Faces Fit!')
HOW IS IT WE DON'T DO SO MUCH BUSINESS WITH THE CHESTER-PERRY ORGANISATION THESE DAYS, MR. PRINGLE?
A FEW YEARS AGO WE SUPPLIED 90% OF THEIR STAFF... THEN ONE DAY WE SLIPPED UP. WE SENT THEM TESS TRELAWNEY....
GO ON...
WHAT DID SHE DO?
WE SHOULD HAVE KNOWN BETTER. THERE WAS SOMETHING STRANGE ABOUT THAT GIRL.........
I WON'T GO INTO DETAILS BUT YOU'VE HEARD OF THE GREAT TEA TROLLEY DISASTER OF '68
YOU MEAN—?
COME WITH ME —I'LL SHOW YOU HER PICTURE....
BLACK MUSEUM
4032

Scene: The offices of Ponsonby's Permanent Positions ('Our Faces Fit!')
MR. PRINGLE—THERE'S A YOUNG LADY HERE WHO'S LOOKING FOR WORK.
AREN'T THEY ALL? WHAT KIND OF WORK?
ANY KIND OF WORK. DOESN'T CARE HOW HARD IT IS.
THAT MAKES A CHANGE... WHAT SALARY IS SHE ASKING?
DOESN'T SEEM TO MIND....
REMARKABLE—LET'S SEE WHAT WE'VE GOT....
CHOICE OF THREE... SIBERIAN SALT MINES, BURMESE RAILWAY OR CHESTER-PERRY TYPING POOL.....
SALT MINES PLEASE
4033

Scene: A police station somewhere in town
HALLO— EAST WINCHLEY POLICE STATION....
WANTED
LOOK OUT —THERE'S A THIEF ABOUT.
CALM DOWN SIR...CALM DOWN
WANTED
LET'S START WITH YOUR NAME, SHALL WE?
YOU ARE MR. BRISTOW OF THE CHESTER-PERRY BUYING DEPARTMENT....
YOU RETURNED FROM LUNCH TODAY TO FIND A SQUARE BROWN ENVELOPE ON YOUR DESK....
...AND YOU'D LIKE US TO SEND A BOMB DISPOSAL EXPERT TO TAKE A LOOK...
WHAT WAS THAT SIR?... YES, IT IS FRIDAY TODAY...
UH HUH... YES, I SUPPOSE IT COULD BE YOUR WAGE PACKET.....
YES, YOU ARE A SILLY OLD CHUMP.......
4045

MORNING, MR. GORDON BLUE
GOOD MORNING. WHAT CAN I DO FOR YOU?
I'M THINKING OF GIVING THE CANTEEN A MISS THIS WEEK IN FAVOUR OF THE PARK. WOULD YOU MIND KNOCKING UP A FEW SANDWICHES— SAY, CHEESE AND PICKLE, ROAST BEEF AND CRISPY BACON?
IN A HAMPER, POSSIBLY?
THAT'S THE IDEA. TWO OF EACH... AND AN APPLE TO FOLLOW. I'LL PICK THEM UP AT LUNCHTIME. THANKS VERY MUCH.
YOU ARE WELCOME.
DOINNG!
3816

CANTEEN
WHAT CAN WE DO? WHAT CAN WE DO?
WITH THIS SUNNY SPELL EVERYONE IS TAKING SANDWICHES TO THE PARK...
WE HAVE TO LURE THEM BACK — BUT HOW?
WE CANNOT IMPROVE UPON THE FOOD OR THE DECOR.. HOW THEN CAN WE ENTICE THEM BACK?
THERE MUST BE SOMETHING WE CAN DO..... SOME ATTRACTION WE CAN OFFER...
TOPLESS WAITRESSES ARE OUT!!!
DAMN! DAMN! DAMN!
3817

WHAT'S WRONG, MR. GORDON BLUE?
NOBODY IS EATING IN THE CANTEEN IN THIS WEATHER... WHAT CAN I DO?
HAND ME THAT MENU.
LET ME SEE...... LIVER SIR REGINALD... STUFFED HEART MASTER ROBIN.... SHOULDER LADY CHESTER PERRY.... BEST END SIR REGINALD...
WHAT COULD BE FINER OR MORE APPETIZING?
JUST NEEDS RE-WORDING TO MAKE IT MORE APPEALING. HOW DOES THIS GRAB YOU?
NOTHING
PLUNGE YOUR KNIFE INTO SIR REGINALD'S BEST END! SINK YOUR TEETH INTO LADY CHESTER-PERRY'S SHOULDER CHOP UP SIR REGINALD'S LIVER! HACK AT MASTER ROBIN'S HEART!
BRAVISSIMO!
3818

'MORNING, MR GORDON BLUE... NICE TO SEE YOU SMILING AGAIN....
YES. TODAY WE ARE EXPECTING A FULL HOUSE.
THOSE OF MY CUSTOMERS WHO HAVE BEEN EATING SANDWICHES IN THE PARK WILL BE RESTORED TO ME.
CONGRATULATIONS.
KEEP YOUR CONGRATULATIONS FOR MY KITCHEN STAFF. THOSE DEAR GIRLS HAVE BEEN HARD AT IT SINCE CRACK OF DAWN...
PREPARING SOME GASTRONOMIC FEAST?
NO — PAINTING EVERY BENCH IN THE PARK.....
3819

MR. GORDON BLUE — WE HAVE A FULL HOUSE.........
AND THEY SHALL EAT AS KINGS.
I HAVE PREPARED A SUPERB COLD BUFFET... WAFER THIN SLICES OF SMOKED SALMON GARNISHED WITH LEMON... CRISP HEARTS OF LETTUCE... FIRM, RIPE TOMATOES....JUICY BEETROOT... CUCUMBER AND WATERCRESS.
STAND ASIDE — LET ME SEE THE ROWS OF SATISFIED FACES
PASS THE TOMATO SAUCE
MAMMA MIA!
ANY MORE TOMATO SAUCE?
AFTER YOU WITH THE TOMATO SAUCE.
IT'S NICE WITH TOMATO SAUCE
TOMATO SAUCE, PLEASE
PASS THE KETCHUP
WHERE'S THE TOMATO SAUCE?
3820

LET'S GET OUT OF HERE BEFORE WE GET CAUGHT.
YOU'RE SO NERVOUS, JONES... WHILE FUDGE IS ON HOLIDAY WE'RE PERFECTLY SAFE....
BUT BRISTOW —
HEY! I'VE HAD A BRAINWAVE
THE REASON FUDGE SEES EVERYTHING WE DO SO EASILY IS BECAUSE OF THAT DOOR.
IF IT OPENED THE OTHER WAY WE'D BE SITTING PRETTY....
I'LL SHOW YOU WHAT I MEAN... PASS ME THAT SCREWDRIVER
YOU'LL BE SO-RRY ♫
FALSETTO! FALSETTO!
3844

COMING TO THE PARK, BRISTOW?
NOT WARM ENOUGH.
BUT THE CHESTER-PERRY WORKS BRASS BAND ARE MAKING THEIR DEBUT AT LUNCHTIME....
WORKS BRASS BAND? I DIDN'T REALISE WE HAD ONE!
YES. THEY'VE BEEN REHEARSING ALL WINTER IN THE PACKING SHED. TODAY THEY'RE GIVING AN OPEN AIR CONCERT IN THE PARK.
THEIR FIRST NUMBER IS 'BABY, IT'S COLD OUTSIDE'..
I REALLY CAN'T STAY..
3768

COME ON, BRISTOW — DON'T BE LIKE THAT. LET'S GO AND GIVE THE CHESTER-PERRY WORKS BRASS BAND A BIT OF SUPPORT ON THEIR DEBUT....
NO THANKS — I'D RATHER NOT...
BUT A LOT OF OUR MATES ARE IN IT... AND I'VE MORE OR LESS PROMISED WE'LL BE THERE...
O.K, O.K... (SIGH!) I SUPPOSE WE MIGHT AS WELL — OTHERWISE WE'LL ONLY HAVE TO FACE THE MUSIC WHEN THEY GET BACK........
3769

HELLO — SOUNDS AS IF THE CHESTER-PERRY BRASS BAND IS ON IT'S WAY...
OOM-PAH! OOM-PAH!
SMART TURNOUT....
OOM-PAH! OOM-PAH!
SOMEONE SAID THE UNIFORM WAS DESIGNED BY SIR REGINALD CHESTER-PERRY HIMSELF.....
FILING CABINET GREEN TUNIC... CLERICAL GREY CAP.. PARCHMENT WHITE SHIRT... INK BLACK TIE... PINSTRIPED TROUSERS... CARBON BLUE SOCKS.........
TWIRL! TWIRL!
CP
CP
3770

SO THAT'S THE CHESTER-PERRY WORKS BRASS BAND, IS IT? WELL, ALL I CAN SAY IS, IF MUSIC BE THE FOOD I'M GLAD I BROUGHT SANDWICHES.
OOMPAH! OOM-PAH!
WHAT DO YOU THINK OF THE CONDUCTOR?
HE'S BEGINNING TO GET ON MY WICK... HE THINKS TOO MUCH OF HIMSELF...
AND NOW, LADIES AND GENTLEMEN, WE SHALL NOW PLAY A NUMBER WHICH I SPECIALLY COMPOSED AND ARRANGED FOR TODAY'S CONCERT. ALTHOUGH I HAVE HAD NO MUSICAL TRAINING....
HARK AT HIM— BLOWING HIS OWN TRUMPET........
3711

LADIES AND GENTLEMEN...THE CHESTER-PERRY WORKS BRASS BAND WILL CONTINUE THEIR OPEN AIR CONCERT WITH A MEDLEY OF POPULAR FAVOURITES..
APRIL SHOWERS
RAINDROPS KEEP FALLING ON MY HEAD.
WHEN YOU WALK THROUGH A STORM
SINGIN' IN THE RAIN...
MUD, MUD, GLORIOUS MUD...
3772

AH, YOUR FEATHERED FRIEND IS BACK.....
MMH!
WHAT A STRANGE EXPRESSION HE HAS ON HIS FACE....
MMMH.....
I USUALLY FEED HIM EVERY MORNING AT THIS TIME BUT TODAY I HAVEN'T BOTHERED...
HE'S PONDERING ON THE VAGARIES OF HUMAN NATURE........
4041

LETTER FOR YOU, MR. STATIONMASTER...
THANK YOU, PERKINS...
BRITISH HI-SPEED RAIL
THIS ENVELOPE SHOULD CONTAIN THE RESULT OF ASSISTANT STATIONMASTER PERKINS' PROMOTION EXAM... —AND I DON'T LIKE THAT CONFIDENT SMILE ON HIS FACE....
THINKS: IF HE'S FAILED— ALL'S WELL...... BUT IF HE'S PASSED THERE COULD BE AN AWKWARD SITUATION... —AND HE SEEMS DEVILISH CONFIDENT
((BREATHE! BREATHE!))
THINKS: UNEASY LIES THE HEAD THAT WEARS A SCRAMBLED EGG CAP......
SLIT! SLIT!
SMIRK! SMIRK!
3987

ASSISTANT STATIONMASTER PERKINS — I HAVE HERE THE RESULT OF YOUR PROMOTION EXAMINATION. IT IS MY SAD DUTY TO INFORM YOU THAT YOU HAVE FAILED MISERABLY...
BRITISH HI-SPEED RAIL
BLANCH! BLANCH!
QUOTE: FAILURE TO DIFFERENTIATE BETWEEN TWO SANDWICHES PICKED UP AT RANDOM FROM THE STATION BUFFET....
GROAN! GROAN!
QUOTE: INSUFFICIENT USE OF UNAUTHORISED HAND SIGNALS WHEN DEALING WITH IRATE PASSENGERS...
MOAN! MOAN!
QUOTE: FAILURE TO READ 'BRITISH HI-SPEED RAIL REGRET EXTENSIVE DELAYS' BOARD AT FIFTY YARDS.... SHALL I GO ON?...
SMIRK! SMIRK!
SOB!
3988

SO YOU FAILED YOUR PROMOTION EXAM, PERKINS —SO WHAT?
BRITISH HI-SPEED RAIL
IN MY BOOK YOU'RE STILL THE BEST ASSISTANT STATIONMASTER I'VE EVER HAD. RAILWAYS ARE IN YOUR VERY BLOOD. YOU ARE PEERLESS IN YOUR CHOSEN FIELD. I HAVE THE UTMOST CONFIDENCE IN YOU....
EEK! THAT NOISE!! THAT DREADFUL NOISE!!!
POOP! POOP!
IT'S ONLY A TRAIN, PERKINS — ONLY A TRAIN........
BROOM CUPBOARD
3989

WHAT THE DEVIL'S GOING ON THIS MORNING, ASSISTANT STATIONMASTER?
8.30 ALREADY AND NO SIGN OF THE 8.15....
I DON'T KNOW — AND WHAT'S MORE I DON'T CARE...
LIKE THAT, IS IT? WHAT'S UP WITH YOU?
BAD NEWS. LAST WEEK I SAT MY PROMOTIONAL EXAM. THIS MORNING THEY TOLD ME I'D FAILED
I'M THINKING OF ENDING IT ALL.... THROWING MYSELF UNDER A TRAIN...
TRAIN? FAT CHANCE ON THIS LINE.......
3990

POOR OLD PERKINS — A BORN LOSER IF EVER I SAW ONE.....
JONES IS ANOTHER... AND DIMKINS...AND HEWITT.... BORN LOSERS ALL.... NONE OF THEM ARE EVER GOING TO GET ANYWHERE...
THEY'LL PLOD ON DAY AFTER DAY, MONTH IN, MONTH OUT, WITH NO CHANCE OF MAKING IT...
IN FACT — TO BE BRUTALLY FRANK, I'M NOT EXACTLY SETTING THE WORLD ON FIRE MYSELF.......
DAMN! DAMN! DAMN! I'M MIXING WITH SO MANY BORN LOSERS SOME OF IT'S RUBBED OFF ON TO ME.......
3991

INVOICE NUMBER 4286/B/231
INVOICE 340181/5 LK/8508
INVOICE 40260 2/9C/2682
YAWN!
INVOICE NUMBER 353/2D/M/9026
INVOICE 2864/8/41
HURL! HURL!
THUD
WHERE DID ALL THE FUN GO?
3786

MR. BRISTOW—HOW LONG HAVE YOU BEEN WITH CHESTER-PERRY'S...?
POSTBOY
FUNNY YOU SHOULD ASK... NINE YEARS TO THIS VERY DAY...
NINE YEARS EH?
NINE YEARS, MAN AND BOY
DO YOU REMEMBER THE ACTUAL DAY YOU JOINED THE FIRM?
DO I REMEMBER? OF COURSE I REMEMBER...
WEDDING OF THE YEAR...
3798

SO YOU'VE BEEN WITH THE FIRM NINE YEARS?
POSTBOY
THAT'S RIGHT, LAD... NINE YEARS TO THIS VERY DAY I SIGNED ON....
NINE YEARS OF PURGATORY.... NINE YEARS OF HELL ON EARTH... NINE YEARS OF SUFFERING... NINE WASTED YEARS...
COME NOW, MR. BRISTOW... NOT EXACTLY WASTED... YOU MUST HAVE LEARNED SOMETHING....
YES
MAKE ONE MISTAKE AND YOU SPEND THE REST OF YOUR LIFE PAYING FOR IT......
3799

THE TROUBLE WITH YOU, MR. BRISTOW, IS YOU'RE SO INDECISIVE...
POST BOY
IF YOU HATE WORKING HERE AS MUCH AS YOU SAY, WHY DON'T YOU PACK IT IN?
WITH THE AMOUNT OF KNOW-HOW YOU'VE PICKED UP SINCE YOU'VE BEEN HERE THERE'S ANY AMOUNT OF JOBS OPEN TO YOU....
RAG AND BONE MAN... BARROW BOY STREET BUSKER... ROAD SWEEPER... JOBBING GARDENER.... ERRAND BOY NIGHT WATCHMAN....
3800

HERE'S A JOB YOU MIGHT BE INTERESTED IN, MR. BRISTOW..... BUYING CLERK WANTED FOR LARGE ENGINEERING FIRM.
NO THANKS. BUYING CLERKS ARE OUT
WHAT ABOUT THIS ONE? LEDGER CLERK REQUIRED.
NOPE.
HOW ABOUT THIS? — WAGES CLERK —
FORGET IT. OFFICE JOBS ARE OUT...
GIVE ME A SHOUT IF YOU COME ACROSS ANY OF THE FOLLOWING —
BRAIN SURGEON. CONCERT PIANIST.. AIRLINE PILOT... ASTRONAUT......
POSTBOY
DAILY THINGS
3801

LET HIM SAY ONE WORD AND I'M OFF...
IF HE THINKS HE CAN TALK TO ME LIKE THAT HE'S GOT ANOTHER THINK COMING...
I'VE STOOD ALL I CAN STAND — ONE WORD OUT OF LINE AND I'LL MAKE HIM SORRY..
I SWEAR IT....
IF THAT POSTBOY SAYS ONE MORE WORD.......
3802

YOU START YOUR HOLIDAYS AT THE END OF THIS WEEK, DON'T YOU?
THAT'S RIGHT....
ARE YOU EXCITED?
NOT SPECIALLY
COME OFF IT, BRISTOW..... I'VE BEEN WATCHING YOU. YOU'VE BEEN WRIGGLING ABOUT ON YOUR SEAT ALL MORNING.....
I'VE MY SWIMSUIT ON UNDERNEATH......
3858

I WONDER WHETHER I'VE MADE A MISTAKE IN RETURNING TO STONEYBEACH FOR MY HOLIDAYS....
THINGS ARE NEVER THE SAME, SECOND TIME AROUND.....
CERTAINLY TRUE OF THIS PLACE — MY WORD, HOW IT'S CHANGED!
THAT'S WHERE THE TOWN HALL USED TO BE......
THAT'S WHERE THE AMUSEMENT ARCADE USED TO BE....
THAT'S WHERE THE BANDSTAND USED TO BE......
THAT'S WHERE THE PIER USED TO BE.......
THAT'S WHERE THE SEA USED TO BE.....
3864

I THINK I MADE A WISE CHOICE IN RETURNING TO THE WESTERBERRY HOTEL...
LIKE MEETING AN OLD FRIEND...
HOW PICTURESQUE — THE HARBOUR BATHED IN THE SETTING SUN...
NOW FOR A GOOD MEAL...I'M STARVING AFTER THAT JOURNEY...
RESTA
I'D LIKE AN AVOCADO WITH SHRIMPS... POACHED TURBOT... AND A CHATEAUBRIAND BEARNAISE WITH FRENCH FRIES, MUSHROOMS, TOMATOES AND —
CAN'T YOU READ??
NO COACH PARTIES
3865

SO FAR SO GOOD...
NICE ROOM OVERLOOKING THE HARBOUR AND AN EXCELLENT MEAL....
AS FINE A START TO A HOLIDAY AS ONE COULD WISH.....
EIGHT FORTY FIVE...
NOW TO HIT THE HIGH SPOTS...
HI THERE — WHERE'S IT ALL AT?
BEG YOUR PARDON SIR?
I SAID 'WHERE'S THE NIGHT LIFE AROUND HERE?'
RECEPTION
WOULD YOU MIND KEEPING YOUR VOICE DOWN, SIR......
EVERYONE HAS GONE TO BED......
3866

OH, BOY...THIS IS THE LIFE... A MAN AT PEACE WITH THE WORLD...
HOW RELAXING TO SIT HERE GAZING AT A BANK OF FLOWERS....
INSTEAD OF SITTING WITH ONE EYE ON THE CLOCK ALL DAY.........
3867

HAPPISNAPS
HAPPISNAPS
ROLL UP! ROLL UP! NO WAITING....
COWBOY KID
P.C.121
CAPTAIN SILVER
CHEESE
CHIEF BUYER
3868

THAT WAS FUN....
I WAS JUST RETURNING FROM A TRIP ROUND THE LIGHTHOUSE — FLAT OUT, ROWING LIKE A GOOD 'UN, WHEN I RAN STRAIGHT INTO THIS OTHER BOAT — KER-UNCH!
WHEN I LOOKED UP THERE WAS THIS BEAUTIFUL BLONDE SPRAWLING IN THE BOTTOM OF HER BOAT...
SHE WAS SOAKED !!
WHAT A DRESSING DOWN SHE GAVE ME! EVERY NAME YOU CAN THINK OF...
THEN OFF SHE WENT IN HIGH DUDGEON...
DON'T KNOW HER NAME OR ANYTHING ABOUT HER...
≡ SIGH! ≡
DOUBT IF WE'LL EVER MEET AGAIN.....
LIKE SHIPS THAT PASS IN THE NIGHT.......
3869

LET ME SEE — WHAT AM I DOING TODAY?
7.30 SWIMMING.
8.0 ROWING...
8.30 MINI GOLF...
9.30 BOWLING
10.0 TENNIS
10.30 FISHING
11.0 SURFING
11.30 DONKEY RIDE... 12.0 PUNCH AND JUDY... 1 P.M. BOAT ROUND THE HARBOUR... 2 P.M. BINGO... 3 P.M. WATER SKIING... 4 P.M. SANDCASTLE COMPETITION... 6 P.M. FUNFAIR... 7 P.M. MYSTERY COACH TOUR 8 P.M. DANCE 9 P.M. MR. STONEYBEACH COMPETITION... 10 P.M. BARBECUE 11 P.M. FIREWORK DISPLAY 12 P.M. MIDNIGHT SWIM...
A FEW MORE DAYS OF THIS AND I'LL BE WELL ON THE WAY TO UNWINDING...
3870

... AND NOW A REQUEST FOR ALL THE WORKERS OF THE CHESTER-PERRY ORGANISATION....
THE REQUEST COMES FROM A MR. BRISTOW WHO IS ON HOLIDAY AT STONEYBEACH SUR LA MER
HE TELLS ME THAT AT THIS VERY MOMENT HE IS SITTING IN A DECKCHAIR IN THE SUN, THINKING OF THOSE ABOUT TO START ON THEIR EIGHT HOUR STINT...
AND THE SONG HE HAS CHOSEN IS 'PUT ON A HAPPY FACE'....
SNARL!
SEETHE!
SEETHE!
GNASH! GNASH!
3871

ONE OF THE PLEASURES OF THE SMALLER SEASIDE RESORT IS HOW QUICKLY ONE GETS TO RECOGNISE PEOPLE....
MORNING
MORNING
MORNING!
I'VE ONLY BEEN HERE A FEW SHORT DAYS AND LOOK AT ME ALREADY...
MORNING!
MORNING!
MORNING!
MORNING!
MORNING!
MORNING!
THERE GOES THE MAN WHO WON THE GIANT TEDDY BEAR AT BINGO LAST NIGHT....
3872

EVERY SEASIDE HAS ONE.....
STAP ME VITALS...
THE OLD SALT ON THE SEA WALL SPINNING YARNS TO THE YOUNGSTERS...
LET'S TARRY A WHILE...
SPLICE THE MAINBRACE... AHOY...
IN MY TIME, SHIPMATES, I'VE HEARD MANY A STRANGE AND TERRIBLE TALE....
BUT TO MY MIND THE MOST BLOODCURDLING STORY OF THEM ALL WAS THE GREAT TEA TROLLEY DISASTER OF '64....
GASP!
SHIVER MY TIMBERS...
3873

VISIT THE WORLD FAMOUS UNDERWATER GROTTO OF STONEYBEACH SEE THE WONDERS OF NATURE! MARVEL AT THE WEIRD ROCK FORMATION.
SNORKELS FOR HIRE.
HOLY
3874

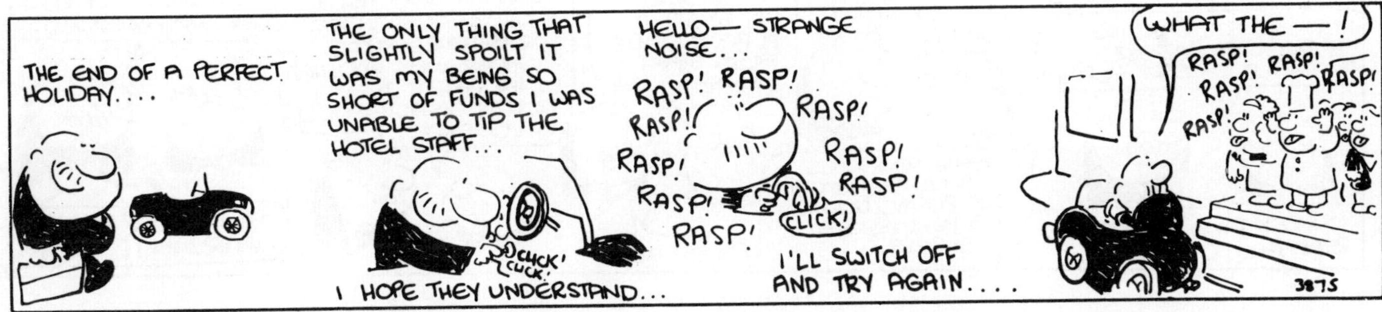

THE END OF A PERFECT HOLIDAY....
THE ONLY THING THAT SLIGHTLY SPOILT IT WAS MY BEING SO SHORT OF FUNDS I WAS UNABLE TO TIP THE HOTEL STAFF...
CLICK! CLICK!
I HOPE THEY UNDERSTAND...
HELLO— STRANGE NOISE...
RASP! RASP! RASP! RASP! RASP! RASP! RASP! RASP! RASP!
CLICK!
I'LL SWITCH OFF AND TRY AGAIN....
WHAT THE —!
RASP! RASP! RASP! RASP! RASP!
3875

Scene: The offices of Messrs Heap and Trotwood, Publishers
'MORNING, MR TASKER. NICE WEEKEND?'
GROAN. DON'T ASK..
HAD TO PLOUGH THROUGH THIS...
'PROFILE OF THE GREATEST LIVING ENGLISHMAN'
SOUNDS INTERESTING
INTERESTING? LISTEN......
'SIR REGINALD CHESTER-PERRY WAS BORN IN..........'
GROAN!
3930

NERVE OF THOSE HACK PUBLISHERS, HEAP & TROTWOOD....
LISTEN TO THIS REJECTION NOTE....
DEAR SIR,
WE ARE RETURNING THE MANUSCRIPT OF YOUR 'PROFILE OF THE GREATEST LIVING ENGLISHMAN' AS WE CAN SEE LITTLE DEMAND FOR A BOOK ON SIR REGINALD CHESTER-PERRY.
YOURS ETC....
Alan Tasker
P.S. WHY DON'T YOU NO-HOPERS GIVE IT A REST?
DEAR SIRS,
IN REPLY TO YOUR OFFENSIVE POSTSCRIPT WE NO-HOPERS SHALL NEVER GIVE IT A REST..
WE SHALL WRITE ON THE BENCHES, WE SHALL WRITE IN UNDERGROUND, WE SHALL WRITE IN THE FIELDS AND IN THE STREETS. WE SHALL WRITE ON THE HILLS..........
3931

HOW ARE YOU ENJOYING MY BIOGRAPHY OF SIR REGINALD CHESTER-PERRY?
YOU CAN TAKE IT BACK — I'VE READ ALL I CAN STAND...
THERE'S NOT A WORD OF TRUTH IN IT....
COME NOW, JONES — A CERTAIN AMOUNT OF POETIC LICENCE IS PERMISSIBLE, SURELY....
POETIC LICENCE MY FOOT! IT'S A PACK OF LIES FROM START TO FINISH....
SUCH AS?
SUCH AS CHAPTER 6. YOUR SUGGESTION THAT OUR BELOVED FIRM'S FOUNDER WAS INVOLVED IN THE GREAT TEA TROLLEY DISASTER OF '68 IS LUDICROUS.
NONSENSE! OF COURSE HE WAS INVOLVED....
HE WAS UP TO HIS EARS IN IT........
3932

AH — TOADY THOMPSON, THE FIRM'S CRAWLER... THE IDEAL PERSON...
WHAT DO YOU THINK OF THIS?
'PROFILE OF THE GREATEST LIVING ENGLISHMAN' WHAT'S IT SUPPOSED TO BE?
IT'S THE MANUSCRIPT OF MY BOOK ON SIR REGINALD CHESTER-PERRY, OUR BELOVED FIRM'S FOUNDER
A BOOK ABOUT SIR REGINALD? WHAT A BRILLIANT IDEA! WHAT A SUBJECT!! IT'LL SELL A MILLION
HEAP AND TROTWOOD REJECTED IT OUTRIGHT
WHAAAT??
A PLAGUE ON BOTH YOUR HOUSES!
3933

WHAT'S UP?
THE REVIEWS OF MY LATEST LITERARY EFFORT, 'PROFILE OF THE GREATEST LIVING ENGLISHMAN'
'..DIFFICULT TO SWALLOW...'.-TEA LADY
'..DOESN'T ADD UP...'.-ATKINS OF ACCOUNTS
'..UNSAVOURY..'.-MR. GORDON BLUE
'..NEEDS POLISHING...' - CLEANING LADY
'..TALL STORY...'-LIFT BOY
BRISTOW — GET SMART...
YOU SPENT FOUR YEARS WRITING 'LIVING DEATH'.. YOU WASTED ANOTHER YEAR ON YOUR POEMS, ANOTHER YEAR ON YOUR HORROR STORIES AND NOW THIS... AND ALL REJECTED... WHY DON'T YOU GIVE UP? YOU'VE OBVIOUSLY NO LITERARY TALENT.
SO WHAT'S WRONG WITH SOMEONE TRYING TO MAKE A FAST BUCK?
3934

BRISTOW — GET ON TO GUN & FAMES RIGHT AWAY AND SORT THIS OUT!
WHY ME? WHY CAN'T HE PICK UP THE 'PHONE HIMSELF?
JUST BECAUSE HE'S CHIEF BUYER...
GET ME GUN & FAMES RIGHT AWAY!
IF I GIVE YOU A LINE WILL YOU GET IT YOURSELF?
WHY SHOULD I? THAT'S WHAT WE PAY YOU FOR!!
3882

Scene: The offices of messrs. Heap and Trottwood, Publishers...
MORNING, MR TASKER, NICE WEEKEND?
DON'T ASK...
I SPENT TWO AND A HALF HOURS OF MY VALUABLE TIME READING THAT RUBBISH...
THUD!
WHAT IS IT?
THERE'S NO TITLE — AND AS FAR AS I'M CONCERNED THERE NEVER WILL BE.....
BAD AS THAT, EH?
BAD AS THAT? — LISTEN...
IT WAS A HOT, SUNNY AFTERNOON AND ALICE WAS MAKING A DAISY CHAIN. SUDDENLY A WHITE COLLAR WORKER HURRIED BY. "I'M LATE" HE SAID, PULLING OUT A POCKET WATCH — AND DISAPPEARED DOWN A SUBWAY.....
GROAN... OFF WITH HIS HEAD...
3810

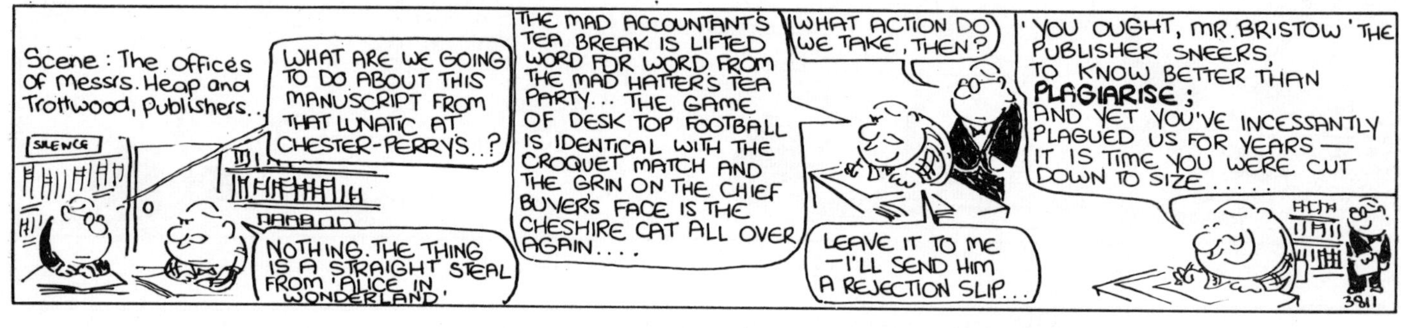

Scene: The offices of messrs. Heap and Trottwood, Publishers...
SILENCE
WHAT ARE WE GOING TO DO ABOUT THIS MANUSCRIPT FROM THAT LUNATIC AT CHESTER-PERRY'S..?
NOTHING. THE THING IS A STRAIGHT STEAL FROM 'ALICE IN WONDERLAND'.
THE MAD ACCOUNTANT'S TEA BREAK IS LIFTED WORD FOR WORD FROM THE MAD HATTER'S TEA PARTY... THE GAME OF DESK TOP FOOTBALL IS IDENTICAL WITH THE CROQUET MATCH AND THE GRIN ON THE CHIEF BUYER'S FACE IS THE CHESHIRE CAT ALL OVER AGAIN....
WHAT ACTION DO WE TAKE, THEN?
LEAVE IT TO ME — I'LL SEND HIM A REJECTION SLIP...
'YOU OUGHT, MR. BRISTOW' THE PUBLISHER SNEERS, 'TO KNOW BETTER THAN PLAGIARISE; AND YET YOU'VE INCESSANTLY PLAGUED US FOR YEARS — IT IS TIME YOU WERE CUT DOWN TO SIZE.....
3811

THE ARROGANCE OF THOSE PUBLISHERS, REJECTING MY LATEST WORK....
NOT ONLY THAT, BUT TO ACCUSE ME OF PLAGIARISING ONE OF LEWIS CARROLL'S BOOKS!
INSOLENT PUPS! I'VE NEVER EVEN HEARD OF THE WOMAN...
RIGHT! I'LL PUT THEM IN THEIR PLACE.... INSULTING MY BOOK LIKE THAT...
DEAR SIRS,
'TWAS BRILLIANT, BUT YOUR HIRED HACKS
DID JEER AND GIGGLE AT MY PROSE
ALL FLIMSY WERE YOUR CHILDISH CRACKS
I'D LIKE TO PUNCH YOUR NOSE.
P.S. BEWARE THE BUYING CLERK, MY SON...
3812

I STILL CAN'T GET OVER THOSE PUBLISHERS ACCUSING ME OF BEING A PLAGIARIST...
LEWIS CARROLL—WHO NEEDS HIM?
I CAN STAND ON MY OWN FEET—I'VE A MILLION IDEAS... LOOK AT THE SIZE OF THAT BRAINBOX..
HOLD IT— INSPIRATION!
STORY ABOUT THIS BUYING CLERK WHO'S LOOKING AT HIMSELF IN THE CLOAKROOM MIRROR...
'WONDER WHAT IT'S LIKE ON THE OTHER SIDE?' HE THOUGHT, AND CLAMBERING UP ON TO THE WASH BASIN HE STEPPED THROUGH THE LOOKING GLASS...
3813

CHEER UP, BRISTOW...
HOW WOULD YOU FEEL IF YOU'D JUST HAD ANOTHER MASTERPIECE REJECTED?
WHY DON'T YOU GIVE UP THE IDEA OF BECOMING A BEST SELLING AUTHOR? WHY NOT BE CONTENTED WITH WHAT YOU ARE?
YOU DON'T UNDERSTAND ME, JONES... I WANT TO BE A BEST SELLING AUTHOR... I WANT MY NAME UP THERE IN LIGHTS... I WANT PEOPLE TO NUDGE EACH OTHER AS I WALK PAST... I WANT THE TRAPPINGS OF SUCCESS... I REALLY WANT ALL THESE THINGS, JONES...
ANYWAY—IT'S NICE TO HAVE A SECOND STRING TO YOUR BOW............
3814.

WONDER HOW OLD POPE, THE FIRM'S HYPOCHONDRIAC, IS FEELING TODAY?
I'LL GIVE HIM A RING... CHEER HIM UP.
POPEY? I'VE WORKED OUT THE ANSWER TO YOUR PROBLEM. IT'S ALL IN THE MIND. YOU MUSTN'T THINK ABOUT ILLNESS EVER AGAIN....
THIS IS BRISTOW, YOU DUM DUM...BRISTOW OF BUYING.... B-R-I-S-T-O-W
B - BRONCHIAL...
R - RHEUMATIC...
I - INSOMNIAC...
S - SUGAR DIABETES...
T - TENNIS ELBOW...
O - OVERWEIGHT...
W - WATER ON THE KNEE...
SOB!
3784.

HAVE YOU SEEN THE NEW BUILDING IN THE CENTRE OF TOWN — MIDDLE APEX?

'FRAID NOT — I'VE BEEN VERY BUSY LATELY... WHAT'S IT LIKE?

IT'S ALREADY BIGGER THAN THE MYLES & RUDGE EXTENSION AND IT'S NOT FINISHED YET. IT SEEMS TO HAVE SPRUNG UP PRACTICALLY OVERNIGHT...

NOT SURPRISING, REALLY... MODERN METHODS OF CONSTRUCTION.... NEW TECHNIQUES.....

THAT'S TRUE.... SOME FIRMS HAVE IT — SOME FIRMS DON'T...
BLONDINI BROTHERS REGRET ANY INCONVENIENCE CAUSED... NOW IN OUR STUPENDOUS 3RD YEAR

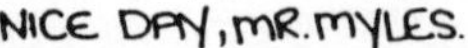

NICE DAY, MR. MYLES...
IS IT, MR. RUDGE? I'M NOT SO SURE....

I'VE BEEN LOOKING AT THE NEW OFFICE BLOCK IN THE CENTRE OF TOWN... MIDDLE APEX......
SO?
IT'S GOING TO BE THIRTY STOREYS...

IS IT, BY JOVE? THAT'LL MAKE IT HIGHER THAN OURS...
A BITTER BLOW MR. RUDGE...

WHAT DO YOU THINK?
WHY NOT INDEED?

ANOTHER THREE PLEASE LADS !!!
BLONDINI BROS (SCAFFOLDING TO THE GENTRY) APOLOGISE FOR ANY...

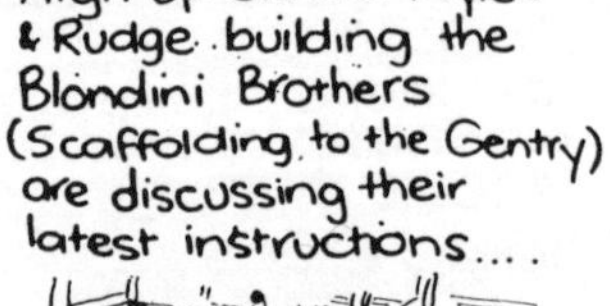

High up on the Myles & Rudge building the Blondini Brothers (Scaffolding to the Gentry) are discussing their latest instructions....

LORDY, LORDY, GEORGE... ANOTHER THREE STOREYS — JUST LIKE THAT...
OURS NOT TO REASON WHY JIM....

METHINKS THIS JOB IS GETTING OUT OF HAND, GEORGE...
NEVER MIND.... WE'LL MANAGE. REMEMBER THE FAMILY MOTTO: UPWARD AND OUTWARD
DOESN'T MEET THE CASE WITH THIS JOB, GEORGE...
THIS IS MORE YOUR PER ARDUA AD ASTRA — THROUGH ADVERSITY TO THE STARS...
HOW APT, JIM.. HOW VERY APT

AT LAST! AT LAST!
THE BLONDINI BROTHERS (SCAFFOLDING TO THE GENTRY) HAVE TAKEN ON EXTRA LABOUR...
LOOK - A ROW OF THEM ALL SITTING ON THAT GIRDER UP THERE...
EXTRA LABOUR MY FOOT!
WOULD YOU BELIEVE - SQUATTERS ALREADY .....?
4014

The story so far : The Blondini Brothers (Scaffolding to the Gentry) have been instructed to add a further 3 storeys to the Myles & Rudge extension.
Word of this reaches mr. Barry Byams, a developer, who is on the site of his new building, Middle Apex...
CURSES! THIS MEANS THE MYLES & RUDGE BUILDING WILL BE THE TALLEST BUILDING IN TOWN...
NO WAY! MY REPUTATION IS AT STAKE — TWO CAN PLAY AT THIS GAME...
ANOTHER FIVE, LADS!!!
4015

WELL, JONES — HOW DO I LOOK IN THE SEAT OF POWER?
BRISTOW — DON'T, PLEASE!
WHAT ABOUT FEET UP?
THUD!
BRISTOW — CUT IT OUT! WHATEVER WOULD FUDGE SAY?
WHO CARES ABOUT FUDGE? LET'S SEE WHAT'S IN THESE DRAWERS... MMH! I MAY HAVE TO FORCE THIS ONE.
TUG! TUG!
BRISTOW!!
EEEK!
IT'S ONLY THE 'PHONE, BRISTOW — ONLY THE PHONE!
BOUND! BOUND!
3843

GOOD LORD—MR. BRISTOW AND MR. JONES! LONG TIME NO SEE......
MENU
HELLO DOLLY...
TRUTH IS, WE'VE BEEN LUNCHING IN THE PARK OF LATE....
BUT NOW THE WEATHER'S TAKEN A TURN FOR THE WORSE WE'VE DECIDED TO EAT IN THE CANTEEN...
RETURN OF THE PRODIGAL AS IT WERE.....
FATTED CALF'S OFF!
3948

ALTHOUGH THE HELPINGS ARE ON THE SMALL SIDE, THIS MEAL IS DELICIOUS. WHERE'S MR GORDON BLUE? I WISH TO CONGRATULATE HIM..
IMPOSSIBLE! OUR MASTER CHEF IS SLEEPING....
EXHAUSTED, NO DOUBT, BY CONSTANT SLAVING OVER A HOT STOVE TO FEED HIS EVER-HUNGRY CLIENTELE..?
NO. OUR BUYER IS ILL AND MR GORDON BLUE HIMSELF WAS UP EARLY THIS MORNING AT THE MARKET....
SCENE.: MEAT MARKET
TIME: 5 AM.
SCRAG END........
3 lb OF MINCE....
1 lb OF PORK SAUSAGES
1 lb STEWING STEAK.....
3949

BONJOUR...BONJOUR...
WELL, WELL... MR. GORDON BLUE, THE MASTER CHEF HIMSELF...
I TRUST YOU ARE ENJOYING TODAY'S SPECIALITY— 'CARBONNADE DE BOEUF ALLA FLAMANDE'
SUPERB!
YOU DO NOT OBJECT BECAUSE THE HELPINGS ARE SMALL?
ON THE CONTRARY — ALL THE MORE ROOM FOR TOMATO SAUCE......
TOMATO SAUCE PLEASE
SHAKE! SHAKE! SHAKE! SHAKE!
SOB!
PASS THE BOTTLE...
AFTER YOU WITH THE TOMATO...
SLURP! SLURP!
3950

WHAT'S UPSETTING MR. GORDON BLUE, OUR MASTER CHEF?
HE'S DESPERATELY TRYING TO THINK OF A WAY TO GET ROUND THIS...
NOW BRING ME ONE DOZEN BOTTLES OF THE BEST COOKING SHERRY... AND A BOTTLE OF FINE BRANDY...
A LEETLE ALCOHOL STIMULATES THE BRAIN...
HE'S ANGRY BECAUSE HIS CUSTOMERS SMOTHER EVERY DISH WITH TOMATO SAUCE....
AH! BRING ME PEN AND PAPER!
YOU HAVE DECIDED ON A DISH?
MAIS NON!
CANTEEN
DO NOT DISTURB
3951

WHY IS MR. GORDON BLUE, OUR MASTER CHEF, LOOKING SO PLEASED WITH HIMSELF?
KNOWING HIS CUSTOMERS' PARTIALITY FOR TOMATO SAUCE HE HAS PREPARED A SPAGHETTI WHICH IS POSITIVELY SMOTHERED IN THE STUFF.....
HERE HE COMES NOW TO GLOAT OVER HIS VICTORY
PASS THE MUSTARD PICKLE....
AFTER YOU WITH THE MUSTARD PICKLE...
SOB!
SUCCESS!
HE HAS PLAYED A MASTERSTROKE....
SHREWD MOVE.. IF YOU CAN'T BEAT 'EM — JOIN 'EM..
LE BOOT IS ON THE OTHER FOOT, NON?
STAND ASIDE, LADIES...
SMIRK! SMIRK!
MUSTARD PICKLE, PLEASE...
LE BITER IS BIT?
OUI!
3952

I LOVE THE AUTUMN MISTS.....
THE OCCASIONAL SHAFT OF SUNLIGHT BREAKING THROUGH...
THE GORGEOUS COLOURS...
THE CRUNCHY, SCRUNCHY UNDERFOOT......
SWIRL!
SWIRL!
SWIRL!
THICKER THE BETTER THEY CAN'T SEE YOU COMING.
ESPECIALLY IF IT SHINES ON A METER SHOWING PENALTY...
'SPECIALLY THE RED OF AN ANGRY FACE WHEN HE DISCOVERS HE'S GOT A TICKET...
DON'T KNOW WHY THEY BOTHER — THEY STILL HAVE TO PAY..........
TICKET
3953

HELLO — WHAT'S GOING ON OVER AT THE ZEBRA CROSSING?
SOUNDS AS IF THE LOLLIPOP LADY IS HAVING A GO AT A MOTORIST...
HOLY COW — IT'S SIR REGINALD CHESTER-PERRY'S ROLLS ROYCE!
STOP
JUST BECAUSE YOU'VE A SWANKY BIG CAR IT DOESN'T MEAN YOU OWN THE ROAD.....ON A ZEBRA CROSSING THE PEDESTRIAN HAS THE RIGHT OF WAY. YOU NEARLY RAN THIS MAN DOWN!
AND DON'T GIVE ME ANY OF YOUR LIP, NEITHER.....I SAW THE WHOLE THING...
...AND IF THIS GENTLEMAN WANTS TO TAKE THE MATTER ANY FURTHER I'LL BE RIGHT BEHIND HIM..........
4023

WHAT WAS ALL THAT HULLABALOO ON THE ZEBRA CROSSING JUST NOW?
THAT LOLLIPOP LADY IS A REAL TARTAR... SHE GAVE SIR REGINALD CHESTER-PERRY, OUR BELOVED FIRM'S FOUNDER, A DRESSING DOWN IN FRONT OF A CROWD OF ONLOOKERS.
REALLY GAVE HIM A TONGUE LASHING..
FROM HENCEFORTH I'LL GIVE HER A WIDE BERTH..
TO ME, LOLLIPOP LADY AND BIG STICK ARE SYNONYMOUS TERMS........
4024

IF YOU ASK ME, JONES — I THINK THE LOLLIPOP LADY —
LISTEN, BRISTOW....I'M FED UP TO HERE WITH LOLLIPOP LADIES
BUT LISTEN, JONES, SHE WAS RIGHT IN STOPPING SIR REGINALD CHESTER-PERRY'S CAR....
BUT HE'S THE FIRM'S FOUNDER!
I DON'T CARE. I AGREE WITH WHAT SHE SAID ABOUT HIM NOT OWNING THE ROAD. AS SHE POINTED OUT, THE FACT THAT HE'S A MULTI-MILLIONAIRE DOESN'T GIVE HIM THE RIGHT TO BREAK THE LAW...
BUT HE PAYS MY WAGES!
I DON'T CARE WHAT HE DOES. HE WAS WRONG AND SHE WAS RIGHT...
I'VE HEARD ENOUGH BRISTOW, TO REALISE THAT THE LOLLIPOP LADY IS LEADING YOU OFF THE STRAIGHT AND NARROW........
4025

I HOPE WORD OF THE ZEBRA CROSSING INCIDENT DOESN'T GET AROUND...
IT WAS EMBARRASSING ENOUGH WITHOUT IT GOING ANY FURTHER...

TO STAND THERE AND HAVE TO LISTEN TO A LOLLIPOP LADY HARANGUING OUR BELOVED FIRM'S FOUNDER WAS MORTIFYING TO SAY THE LEAST...
STAFF ENTRANCE

WHAT'S BLACK AND WHITE AND RED ALL OVER?

BRISTOW ON A ZEBRA CROSSING...
LIKE IT LIKE IT
WE ARE NOT AMUSED...
4027

HERE YOU ARE, MR. B... NICE CUP OF TEA AND ONE OF MY HOME MADE LIGHT-AS-A-FEATHER FAIRY CAKES...
YOU'RE TOO KIND.

NICE CUP OF TEA...

BUT I'M NOT TOO SURE ABOUT HER HOME MADE LIGHT-AS-A-FEATHER FAIRY CAKES...

HOW MUCH DOES LEAD FETCH ON THE OPEN MARKET?
WEIGH WEIGH!
3785

RIGHT. AFTER ME......
NO, NO—YOU'RE FLAT... THROW YOUR HEAD BACK AND OPEN YOUR BEAK.... NOW. AFTER ME...
NO, NO, NO... YOU'RE FLAT....
PAY ATTENTION!
WHAT'S GOING ON?
I'M TRAINING HIM TO SING LIKE A NIGHTINGALE.....
3809

'MORNING, BRISTOW — MAY I HAVE A WORD WITH YOU?
FIRE AWAY, HICKFORD..
IT'S ABOUT THIS ARTICLE YOU'VE SUBMITTED FOR THE HOUSE JOURNAL...
SNATCH!
AH, YES. WELL, HAVING LIVED WITH THIS PROJECT FOR SEVERAL YEARS I ENVISAGE A DOUBLE PAGE CENTRE SPREAD WITH PHOTOGRAPHS ARRANGED THUS...
I'M AFRAID IT ISN'T THAT SIMPLE — WE'RE REJECTING IT....
GASP! YOU'RE TURNING IT DOWN ??
TURNING IT DOWN FLAT!
YOU SEE, A VITRIOLIC ATTACK ON THE FIRM'S FOUNDER DOESN'T QUITE FIT IN WITH HOUSE JOURNAL POLICY......
MAN'S INHUMANITY TO MAN....
3792

WOE, WOE, WOE......
TO THINK AN ARTICLE OF MINE WAS REJECTED BY THE HOUSE JOURNAL....
THE ULTIMATE DEGRADATION...
THAT SOULLESS PIG OF AN EDITOR HAS DESTROYED MY EVERY HOPE OF A LITERARY CAREER......
I'LL MAKE HIM SORRY, JUST WAIT AND SEE...
WHERE'S MY PEN AND PAPER?
IT IS A FAR, FAR BETTER THING THAT I DO THAN I HAVE EVER DONE; IT IS A FAR, FAR BETTER REST I GO TO THAN I HAVE EVER KNOWN........
3793

GASP! GRUNT!
SWEAT! SWEAT! STRAIN! STRAIN!
GROAN! GROAN! PUFF! PUFF!
IT'S NO USE — I GIVE UP....
SURELY THERE'S AN EASIER WAY OF COMMITTING SUICIDE THAN WORKING ONESELF TO DEATH....
3794

IT'S NO USE — I'LL NEVER BE ABLE TO COMMIT SUICIDE BY WORKING MYSELF TO DEATH...
I'LL HAVE TO END IT ALL ANOTHER WAY....
I WANT SOMETHING PAINLESS AND QUICK...
GET ON WITH YOUR WORK!!
WISH HE WOULDN'T DO THAT.....
FRIGHTENED THE LIFE OUT OF ME.....
3795

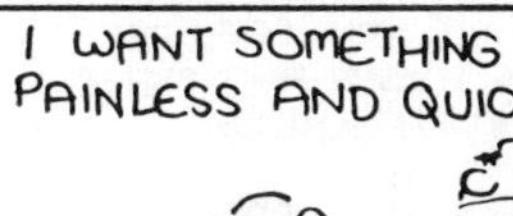

BRISTOW — I THINK YOU'RE SILLY TO GET DEPRESSED SIMPLY BECAUSE THE HOUSE JOURNAL REJECTED YOUR ARTICLE....
IT'S ALL RIGHT FOR YOU.
IN A WAY IT'S A GOOD THING...
ALL THE BEST PEOPLE HAVE HAD THEIR WORK REJECTED BY THEIR HOUSE JOURNAL AT SOME TIME OR OTHER..
CHARLES DICKENS... TOLSTOY... GALSWORTHY.. JANE AUSTEN.. BERNARD SHAW... THE BRONTËS — ALL TURNED DOWN BY THEIR HOUSE JOURNALS.....
REALLY.?
WELL KNOWN FACT. FEELING BETTER? AGATHA CHRISTIE... IAN FLEMING... DENNIS WHEATLEY ..TENNESSEE WILLIAMS LESLIE CHARTERIS...P.G.WODEHOUSE....
37%

AT THIS VERY MOMENT SIR REGINALD CHESTER-PERRY, OUR BELOVED FIRM'S FOUNDER, WILL BE SETTING SAIL FOR THE BAHAMAS...
LUCKY DEVIL.
I DON'T KNOW..... DOESN'T LOOK ALL THAT PROMISING OUT THERE... BLEAK AND COLD
SHOULDN'T BE SURPRISED IF WE ARE IN FOR A STORM.
WE ARE... LISTEN TO THAT THUNDER....
RUMBLE! RUMBLE!
EVERYBODY REPORT TO RECEPTION. AT ONCE!
FOR THOSE IN PERIL ON THE SEA
3917

WHAT A GLORIOUS MORNING!
THE CRISP AIR AND THE SCRUNCH OF LEAVES UNDERFOOT...
SCRUNCH!
SCRUNCH! SCRUNCH! SCRUNCH!
MY TIME OF YEAR, THIS... WHAT WAS IT THE POET KEATS SAID?
SCRUNCH! SCRUNCH!
SCRUNCH! SCRUNCH! SCRUNCH! SCRUNCH! SCRUNCH!
AUTUMN, SEASON OF MISTS AND MELLOW FRUITFULNESS....
STATION
BRITISH HI-SPEED RAIL REGRET DELAYS DUE TO
Mists and mellow fruitfulness
3936

TUT, TUT — THESE DELAYS DO NOTHING FOR THE IMAGE OF BRITISH HI-SPEED RAIL...
STATION MASTER
TIMETABLE
ASSISTANT STATIONMASTER PERKINS CAN TAKE OVER THE OFFICE FOR A SPELL...
I SHALL STROLL ALONG THE PLATFORM AND PACIFY THE PASSENGERS....
WHERE IS MY STATION-MASTER'S WINTER GREATCOAT?
—AND COME TO THINK OF IT, WHERE THE DEVIL IS PERKINS?
PERKINS IS NOT FAR AWAY:
3 POSES FOR 10P
3937

LISTEN TO THOSE PASSENGERS OUT THERE, SIR....
HI-SPEED RAIL
I DON'T BLAME THEM, PERKINS. IT'S ALREADY 8.33 AND NO SIGN OF THE 8.15 COMMUTER SPECIAL....
I DON'T LIKE THE LOOK OF IT, SIR. THEY'VE STARTED BREAKING UP THE BENCHES AND SMASHING WINDOWS...
WHAAAT?
PERKINS — GO OUT THERE AND HUMOUR THEM!
BUT SIR—!
DON'T ARGUE, PERKINS —THAT'S AN ORDER....
AND REMEMBER.... STICKS AND STONES MAY BREAK YOUR BONES..........
PROPEL! PROPEL!
3938

HELLO — THIS IS THE STATIONMASTER, EAST WINCHLEY... HOW MUCH LONGER HAVE WE TO WAIT FOR THE 8.15 COMMUTER SPECIAL?
CAN'T SAY....
BUT IT'S ALREADY 8.35 AND TEMPERS ARE BEGINNING TO FRAY...
I'VE HAD TO SEND ASSISTANT STATIONMASTER PERKINS OUT ON TO THE PLATFORM TO REASON WITH THE PASSENGERS.....
SHOULDN'T BE LONG, ANYWAY.
I SHOULD HOPE NOT. THE NATIVES ARE GETTING RESTLESS....
SO YOU KEEP SAYING. EXACTLY HOW RESTLESS ARE THEY?
WELL — THEY'VE GOT PERKINS......
GET A ROPE!
3939

STATIONMASTER, EAST WINCHLEY REPORTING. THE 8.15 COMMUTER SPECIAL FINALLY LEFT FROM HERE AT 8.45, AFTER SEVERAL UGLY SCENES ON THE PLATFORM...
BRITISH HI-SPEED RAIL SCHEDULE
THINGS LOOKED SO GRIM AT ONE STAGE I HAD TO SEND ASSISTANT STATIONMASTER PERKINS OUT TO REASON WITH THEM....
THANK YOU SIR — GOOD MORNING!
NOW THEN — WHAT'S TO BE DONE?
AH, YES.......
RELEASE POOR PERKINS.........
SNAP!
3940

WINTER DRAWS NIGH AND MY FEATHERED FRIEND IS UNSETTLED...
FIDGET! FIDGET!
SEE HOW RESTLESS HE IS... A PRIMAL FORCE IS TUGGING HIM.... SOMEWHERE OUT THERE A VOICE IS CALLING, CALLING... COME AWAY...COME AWAY...
BRISTOW — HOW MANY TIMES MUST I TELL YOU? — COME AWAY FROM THAT WINDOW !!!!
3935

GUN & FAMES? THIS IS BRISTOW OF CHESTER-PERRYS..
MORNING MR. BRISTOW HOW'S THINGS?
LOUSY. HOW ARE THINGS WITH YOU?
TERRIBLE! WE'VE A NEW MAN AT THE TOP. BIT OF A DISCIPLINARIAN....
AS A RESULT THINGS ARE TIGHTENING UP.
REALLY?
I'LL SAY. DO YOU KNOW THEY'VE EVEN PUT A SIGN IN THE FOYER 'NO CYCLING. DOGS MUST BE KEPT ON A LEAD. NO TRANSISTORS....'
MAN'S INHUMANITY TO MAN....
3883

SO THINGS ARE NOT SO FREE AND EASY AT GUN AND FAMES THESE DAYS?
I'LL SAY THEY'RE NOT...
WE HAVE TO ARRIVE AND LEAVE AT SPECIFIED TIMES....
GOOD HEAVENS!
WE HAVE TO WEAR A COLLAR AND TIE..
THE MIND BOGGLES
WE HAVE TO WAIT UNTIL PAYDAY FOR OUR WAGES.........
MAN'S INHUMANITY TO MAN.......
3884

GUESS WHAT — GUN & FAMES ARE HAVING TO TOE THE LINE AT LAST!
WHAAAT?
THEY'RE ACTUALLY HAVING TO EARN THEIR MONEY..
YOU'RE KIDDING!
NO — HONESTLY....I'VE JUST BEEN SPEAKING TO THEM.
THEY'VE EVEN TAKEN TO WEARING SUITS AND CLOCKING IN AND OUT.....
LINE PLEASE...
SELL MY GOLD SHARES — BUY GUN AND FAMES....
3885

I DIDN'T REALISE YOU PLAYED THE MARKET, JONES..
DO YOU MAKE ANY MONEY AT IT?
WHO ADVISES YOU?
WHAT STOCK DO YOU HAVE IN YOUR PORTFOLIO AT THE MOMENT?
ROLLS RAZOR... FIRE & MARINE AUTO. VEHICLE & GENERAL
LUCKY DEVIL!!
THERE ARE MANY THINGS ABOUT ME OF WHICH YOU ARE IGNORANT, BRISTOW...
SMIRK! SMIRK!
THAT'D BE TELLING....
NOBODY. I PLAY MY HUNCHES.
3886

RUN! RUN! RUN!
FIRE?
NO!
BOMB SCARE?
NO
BUYING DEPARTMENT ARE CASTING FOR THEIR NATIVITY PLAY.....
RUN! RUN! RUN!
3954

WHAT ARE YOU DOING, JONES?
SEE THAT BENT TEASPOON? I DID THAT BY CONCENTRATION...
I'M TRYING TO BEND THE HANDS OF THE OFFICE CLOCK...... CONCENTRATE!...... CONCENTRATE!
THERE — I'VE DONE IT! BIG HAND ON THE TWELVE — SMALL HAND ON THE FIVE ....
G'NIGHT ALL!
I'M DOING A URI GELLER...
INCREDIBLE. WHAT'S YOUR NEXT TRICK?
4010

'MORNING, BRISTOW...
SHUT UP, YOU...
DOWN IN THE DUMPS, ARE YOU?
GET LOST....
BE LIKE THAT, THEN..
WHAT'S UP WITH HIM?
THE MORNING AFTER THE DAY BEFORE......
3941

'TWAS ON A MONDAY MO-ORNING WHEN I BEHELD MY DA-ARLING
SHE LOOKED SO NEAT AND CHA-ARMING IN EVERY HIGH DEGREE...
SHE LOOKED SO NEAT AND NIMBLE O A-CLEANING OF THE PHONIO...
RUBBING AWAY WITH HER CLEANING CLOTH.
3852

COME AND LOOK AT THIS, JONES.....
HAVE YOU EVER SEEN SUCH A VISION?
WHERE'S THE VISION? ALL I CAN SEE IS THE KLEENAPHONE GIRL.....
SUCH GRACE, SUCH MOVEMENT!
MUST BE ON PIECEWORK
WHAT A PICTURE SHE MAKES.... LIKE A TITIAN...
BLESS YOU
LOOK AT THOSE COLOURS
SHE COULD DO WITH A CLEAN DUSTER
AND ALL AROUND HER A GOLDEN HALO....
TOO HEAVY HANDED WITH HER DISINFECTANT SPRAY.....
3853

MEMO FROM ACCOUNTS DEPARTMENT.....
EXCUSE ME, PLEASE...
THANK YOU!
SIGH!
EXTRAORDINARY BEHAVIOUR — WHAT DO YOU MAKE OF IT?
MISS PRETTY OF KLEENAPHONE MUST BE WORKING HER WAY ALONG THE SECOND FLOOR OF THE BUILDING OPPOSITE......
3855

THERE SHE GOES...
SIGH!
THE GORGEOUS MISS PRETTY OF KLEENAPHONE...
HOW FRAGILE AND FEMININE SHE LOOKS AS SHE EMERGES FROM THE MYLES & RUDGE BUILDING.......
STEPS GRACEFULLY INTO HER LITTLE PINK KLEENAPHONE VAN....
AND ZIG ZAGS AWAY INTO THE SUNSET......
3856

SWITCHBOARD.
IS THAT YOU, MARY.?
I WONDER WHETHER YOU CAN DO ME A FAVOUR. COULD YOU KNIT ME A LITTLE HOOD?
TODDLER SIZE?
NO. SMALLER.
BABY SIZE?
SMALLER STILL.
WHAT SIZE, EXACTLY?
DIFFICULT TO SAY.....
3857

ONLY SEVEN MORE DAYS OF FREEDOM...
WHAT SHALL WE DO THIS MORNING?
DESK TOP FOOTBALL?
YOU'RE ON.
RIGHT?
IN FUDGE'S OFFICE.....
NOT HERE, DUM DUM...
YOU MEAN—?
EXACTLY— THE SACRED TURF!
FREDERICK J. FUDGE CHIEF BUYER
3840

OLD FUDGE WOULD FOAM AT THE MOUTH IF HE KNEW WE WERE PLAYING DESK TOP FOOTBALL IN HIS OFFICE... ON HIS ACTUAL DESK!
O.K... LET'S GO! ARSENAL TO KICK OFF...
WHAT'S THE MATTER WITH YOU? WHY ARE YOU STANDING THERE LIKE THAT?
WHENEVER I'M IN THIS OFFICE I AUTOMATICALLY TAKE UP THIS POSITION...........
3841

DOESN'T IT STRIKE YOU AS FUNNY, JONES, THAT FUDGE'S DESK TOP IS ABSOLUTELY UNMARKED?
ACRE UPON ACRE OF POLISHED WOOD AND LEATHER....
I COULDN'T SIT BEHIND A DESK LIKE THIS ALL DAY... TO ME IT DOESN'T LOOK LIVED IN....
LEND ME YOUR PENKNIFE...
NOW THEN — WHAT ARE YOUR INITIALS AGAIN?
3842

JONES — I'M SELLING TICKETS FOR THE FIRM'S CHRISTMAS DINNER AND DANCE NEXT WEEK
COAX ME
DO YOU WANT THE HARD SELL OR THE SOFT SELL?
WHAT'S THE DIFFERENCE?
THE HARD SELL STARTS WITH A SMACK IN THE MOUTH.
WHAT TIME NEXT WEEK?
3955

AH, LIFT BOY — JUST THE LAD I WANTED TO SEE....
I'M SELLING TICKETS FOR THE FIRM'S CHRISTMAS DANCE...
NO THANKS. YOU KNOW WHAT YOU CAN DO WITH YOUR MILITARY TWO STEP AND YOUR VALETA.
NO NO — IT'S GOING TO BE DIFFERENT THIS YEAR. IT'S FOCUS ON YOUTH.....
REGGAE? SOUL? MASH? FUNKY CHICKEN? BOOGALOO? HITCH HIKER?
NATCH!
WHAT ELSE? ER...JITTERBUG...ER... SIMPLE SIMON... ER.. WALTZ.. ER...TANGO...
KEEP GOING..
ER... FOXTROT.. QUICK-STEP... GAY GORDON... ER..... MILITARY TWO STEP... VALETA.....
3956

JUST THE MAN I WANTED TO SEE....
IT'S THE FIRM'S CHRISTMAS DINNER AND DANCE NEXT FRIDAY. I'M SELLING TICKETS. HOW MANY DO YOU WANT?
WELL — TO TELL THE TRUTH OLD MAN, I DOUBT WHETHER —
IT'LL BE A WONDERFUL NIGHT —
SUPERB FOOD... CHOICE WINES, DANCING, CABARET, SPOT PRIZES, A RAFFLE...
A CHANCE TO RENEW OLD FRIENDSHIPS AND MEET NEW FACES... AN EVENING OF CONVIVIALITY AND WARMTH...
I'LL TAKE TWO. SAY — YOU'RE REALLY TRYING TO GET THIS THING OFF THE GROUND, EH?
NO! IF I SELL MORE THAN FIFTEEN TICKETS I DON'T HAVE TO GO...
3957

GOODNIGHT ALL...
WHERE DO YOU THINK YOU'RE GOING? IT'S ONLY TEN TO FIVE...
TIME OFF FOR GOOD BEHAVIOUR
SLAM!
3966

IT'S LIKE GRAND CENTRAL STATION IN HERE THESE DAYS... WHAT'S GOING ON?
ONCE BUYING DEPARTMENT ANNOUNCED THEY'D STOPPED CASTING THEIR NATIVITY PLAY PEOPLE BEGAN APPEARING OUT OF THE WOODWORK......
3967

I'D LIKE TO SPEAK TO MR BRISTOW OF BUYING....
SPEAKING.
THIS IS JACKSON OF GUN & FAMES...
I WONDER, COULD YOU GIVE ME YOUR HOME ADDRESS...?
SORRY. IT'S AGAINST COMPANY POLICY. ANY PERSONAL GIFTS HAVE TO BE ADDRESSED TO ME AT THE FIRM....
I WASN'T THINKING OF A GIFT....
I WAS THINKING OF SPENDING CHRISTMAS AT YOUR PLACE....
NO WAY....
3968

ON THE EIGHTH DAY OF CHRISTMAS SIR REGGIE SAID TO ME — EIGHT FIRMS A WAITING SEVEN PHONES A RINGING SIX ORDERS PENDING
FIVE STOLEN MINS.
Z
GET ON WITH IT!
FOUR GALLING WORDS THREE DRY PENS
SQUEAK! SQUEAK!
TWO TWIDDLING THUMBS
AND AN INVOICE IN AN IN-TRAY
3969

I'M ASTONISHED....I DIDN'T REALISE BRISTOW OF BUYING HAD DEALINGS WITH SO MANY OTHER FIRMS...
HIS OFFICE IS FULL OF CHRISTMAS CARDS... HUNDREDS AND HUNDREDS OF THEM....
I KNOW A LOT OF FIRMS SEND OUT CARDS AS A DUTY BUT EVEN SO....
AUNT EMILY, UNCLE FRANK, AUNT AGNES AND THE CHILDREN, COUSIN JOAN, THE DOYLE FAMILY, MIKE, JANET AND THE KIDS, MR & MRS KELLY........
3970

YIPPEE!!
CLICK!
THE MANAGEMENT HAVE REALLY GOT THE CHRISTMAS SPIRIT.....
SKIP! SKIP! SKIP!
THIS YEAR WE'RE GETTING DECEMBER 25TH OFF......
SKIP! SKIP! SKIP!
SKIP
3971

HERE'S THE SEATING PLAN FOR TONIGHT'S DINNER AND DANCE...
DO TELL!
DO TELL..
JONES, LUCKY DOG, IS NEXT TO NATALIE THE FIRM'S SEXPOT...
WOW!
HEWITT, FORTUNATE FELLOW, IS NEXT TO MR. SHARMAN, THE FIRM'S TOTAL ABSTAINER...
YIPPEE!
PILKINGTON IS IN FOR A GOOD TIME —HE'S GOT MR. GABBY, THE FIRM'S RACONTEUR...
WHAT ABOUT ME?
BAD NEWS..... FATTY STEADMAN, THE FIRM'S PIG....
TAKE SANDWICHES
3961

WELL, WELL, CHRISTMAS CRACKERS, EH?
PRESENT FROM THE MANAGEMENT....
DINNER DANCE
"EACH CRACKER CONTAINS A PARTY HAT AND A MOTTO..."
TUG! TUG!
BANG! BANG! BANG!
REPENT, YE SINNER
MONEY IS THE ROOT OF ALL EVIL..
BUSINESS BEFORE PLEASURE...
VIRTUE IS IT'S OWN REWARD
3962

HELLO — THERE'S A DISTURBANCE OVER BY THE DOOR...
NOTHING TO WORRY ABOUT.... GATE CRASHERS..
COME ON, LADS — LET'S SORT THEM OUT——
NOBODY GETS IN TO OUR FIRM'S PARTY...
THEY'RE NOT TRYING TO GET IN, DUM DUM — THEY'RE TRYING TO GET OUT!!
JC
3963

RUN! RUN! RUN!
WHAT'S THE RUSH?
SPECIAL CHRISTMAS LUNCH IN THE FIRM'S CANTEEN....
RUMOUR HAS IT LUCKY ONES WILL FIND THEIR ANNUAL BONUS IN THE CHRISTMAS PUDDING.......
3974

SEEN THE NOTICE BOARD?
NOT YET....
THE ANNUAL CHRISTMAS MESSAGE OF GOOD WILL FROM THE MANAGEMENT. IT SAYS —
DON'T TELL ME —
I KNOW IT BY HEART....
ANY EMPLOYEE CAUGHT BRINGING ALCOHOLIC BEVERAGES INTO THE BUILDING WILL BE LIABLE TO INSTANT DISMISSAL......
WORD PERFECT!
3975

O LITTLE TOWN OF BETHLEHEM HOW STILL WE SEE THEE LIE...
CHESTER-PERRY GLEE CLUB CAROL PRACTICE
ABOVE THY DEEP AND DREAMLESS SLEEP THE SILENT STARS GO BY...
YET IN THY DARK STREETS SHINETH THE EVERLASTING LIGHT
2½ HOURS OVERTIME AT TIME AND A THIRD...
3976

HOW DID LAST NIGHT'S DINNER AND DANCE GO?
WAS SIR REGINALD CHESTER-PERRY THERE?
MADE HIS USUAL BORING SPEECH, I SUPPOSE?
EVERY TIME HE OPENED HIS MOUTH TO SPEAK HIS VOICE WAS DROWNED BY BREAD ROLLS WHISTLING THROUGH THE AIR.....
GREAT. BEST YET...
NO. OLD MAN PETTIGREW FILLED IN FOR HIM...
I BELIEVE HE TRIED SEVERAL TIMES...
LIKE IT! LIKE IT!
3965

I HATE IT! I HATE IT!
I'M AFRAID YOU'VE GOT TO GRIT YOUR TEETH AND BEAR IT....
CHRISTMAS AFFECTS SOME PEOPLE THIS WAY......
DON'T WORRY — THIS IS THE WORST PART... IT'LL SOON BE OVER...
TRAFFIC WARDEN
RIP!
RIP!
RIP!
3972

HO! HO! HO! MERRY CHRISTMAS... HO! HO! HO!
I'VE GOT TO HAND IT TO YOU, BRISTOW.... YOU REALLY ARE GREAT FUN TO HAVE AROUND THE OFFICE AT THIS TIME OF YEAR..
YOU ENTER INTO THE SPIRIT OF THINGS... JUST AS THE CHRISTMAS RUSH WAS BEGINNING TO GET ME DOWN, THERE YOU ARE PLAYING THE FOOL TO CHEER ME UP...
TO HELL WITH THE WORK — I'LL SIT DOWN AND RELAX...
SOMEONE'S TAKEN THE STUFFING OUT OF MY CUSHION!
HO! HO! HO!
HO! HO! HO!
HO! HO! HO!
HO! HO! HO! MERRY CHRISTMAS!
3973